Collins

KS3
Science
Year 9

Ian Honeysett, Sam Holyman and Lynn Pharaoh

How to use this book

Each Year 9 topic is presented on a two-page spread

Organise your knowledge with concise explanations and examples

Key points highlight fundamental ideas

Test your retrieval skills by trying the accompanying questions for the topic

Mixed questions further test retrieval skills after all topics have been covered

Scientific skills section provides further knowledge and explanations of scientific ideas and investigative skills

Answers are provided to all questions at the back of the book

ACKNOWLEDGEMENTS

The authors and publisher are grateful to the copyright holders for permission to use quoted materials and images.

Every effort has been made to trace copyright holders and obtain their permission for the use of copyright material. The authors and publisher will gladly receive information enabling them to rectify any error or omission in subsequent editions. All facts are correct at time of going to press.

All images ©Shutterstock and HarperCollins*Publishers*

Published by Collins
An imprint of HarperCollins*Publishers* Limited
1 London Bridge Street
London SE1 9GF

HarperCollins*Publishers*
Macken House, 39/40 Mayor Street Upper,
Dublin 1, D01 C9W8, Ireland

© HarperCollins*Publishers* Limited 2023

ISBN 9780008598693

First published 2023

10 9 8 7 6 5 4 3 2

British Library Cataloguing in Publication Data.

A CIP record of this book is available from the British Library.

Authors: Ian Honeysett, Sam Holyman and Lynn Pharaoh
Publisher: Clare Souza
Commissioning: Richard Toms
Project Management: Katie Galloway
Inside Concept Design: Ian Wrigley
Layout: Rose & Thorn Creative Services Ltd
Cover Design: Sarah Duxbury
Production: Emma Wood
Printed and bound in the UK

MIX
Paper | Supporting responsible forestry
FSC
www.fsc.org
FSC™ C007454

This book is produced from independently certified FSC™ paper to ensure responsible forest management.

For more information visit:
www.harpercollins.co.uk/green

Contents

(1) What is variation?

Biodiversity and classification

Scientists estimate that there are about 9 million different types of organisms living on Earth today:
- all organisms live together in different ecosystems and rely on each other
- this large variety of organisms is called **biodiversity**.

> A high biodiversity usually means a healthy and stable ecosystem.

Scientists put all organisms into groups. This is called **classification**. Modern classification puts organisms into groups based on the number of common characteristics that they share. This allows scientists to:
- make predictions about the characteristics of newly discovered organisms
- work out which organisms are most closely related to each other.

The classification system used today has different size groups. The smaller the number of organisms in a group then the more similar they are. The smallest group is called a **species**. All the members of a species are similar enough to breed with each other to produce fertile offspring. For example, lions, tigers and cats share a number of features and are classified together in a large group. However, they are different species as they cannot interbreed to produce fertile offspring.

Causes of variation

Even in one species there are differences between organisms. This is called **variation**. Variation between organisms can be caused by:
- inherited characteristics from their parents
- the environment they live in
- a combination of inherited factors and the environment.

Types of variation

In some types of variation, only a certain number of characteristics can exist. There are no in-between values. This is called **discontinuous variation**. An example is found in human blood groups.

In other types of variation, all possible characteristics in a range are possible. This is called **continuous variation**. An example is the height of children in a class.

> Discontinuous variation is often caused by inherited factors. Continuous variation is usually controlled by the environment or a combination of inheritance and the environment.

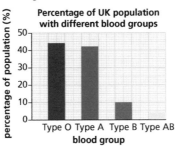

Percentage of UK population with different blood groups

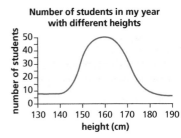

Number of students in my year with different heights

1) What is variation?

Biodiversity and classification

1 Give the scientific term that is described by each definition.

a) A group of organisms that can interbreed to produce fertile offspring. ....

b) The variety of different organisms living in an ecosystem. ....

c) The process of sorting organisms into groups. ....

2 Horses and donkeys can mate to produce a mule. Mules are infertile.

What does this tell you about horses and donkeys?

....

Causes of variation

3 The table lists some examples of variation in human characteristics.

Put one tick in each row of the table to show the cause of the variation.

Example	Inherited	Environment	Inherited and environment
a scar on the cheek			
blood group			
human height			
sex at birth			

4 Explain why identical twins often look different when they are teenagers, but not when they are five years old.

....

....

Types of variation

5 The graph shows the shoe sizes of all the students in a class.

a) How many students are in the class?

....

b) What is the most common shoe size?

....

c) What type of variation is shown in the graph?

....

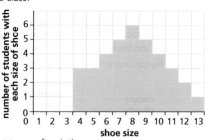

d) Explain why shoe size and foot size show different types of variation.

....

....

....

What is the difference between natural selection and artificial selection?

ORGANISE 1

Natural selection and evolution

For many years, scientists have realised that populations of organisms can change over long periods of time. This is **evolution**.

Many theories have been put forward to try to explain how evolution may have happened. Most scientists now support the theory put forward by **Charles Darwin** in his famous book published in 1859. He called his theory **natural selection**.

This is how natural selection works:

- All organisms are slightly different, showing variation.
- The organisms compete with each other.
- The organisms that are best suited to the environment survive.
- These surviving organisms pass on their characteristics.
- Over many years the population of organisms will change.

> Over long enough periods of time, natural selection can produce new species.

Artificial selection

For centuries before Darwin, farmers have been changing the characteristics of plant and animal populations through **artificial selection** (selective breeding). This is how it works:

- Farmers decide what characteristic they want in their animals or crops.
- They choose the individuals that best show those characteristics.
- *These individuals are then allowed to breed together.*
- This process is continued with the offspring for generations.

Both artificial selection and natural selection cause changes in populations but there are differences:

Some cattle have been bred to produce high yields of milk. Most cows produce five gallons; two in the herd produce six. The two that produce six gallons are used to breed from.

Artificial selection	Natural selection
• Can happen quickly. • Humans choose which organisms reproduce. • The offspring produced are often less fit and healthy.	• Often takes thousands of years. • The environment chooses which organisms reproduce. • The offspring produced are fitter and healthier.

Extinction

When there are no more individuals of a species left alive in the world, they are described as **extinct**. Extinction is a natural process that happens due to natural selection. Organisms that are less well adapted are less likely to survive and reproduce so the species dies out.

However, humans have increased the rate of extinction in different ways:

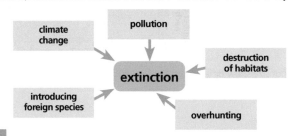

climate change
pollution
destruction of habitats
extinction
introducing foreign species
overhunting

the dodo became extinct in the late 1600s

What is the difference between natural selection and artificial selection?

Natural selection and evolution

1 Complete these sentences by writing the correct words in the gaps.

Populations of organisms change over time and this change is called ....

A scientist called .... put forward a generally accepted theory to explain this

process. He called the theory ....

2 Some people use the phrase 'survival of the fittest' to describe the process of evolution.

Which of these statements gives the best description of 'fittest' in evolution? Tick the correct answer.

Organisms that have the largest muscles ☐

Organisms that are best suited to their environment ☐

Organisms that can run, eat or fly the fastest ☐

Artificial selection

3 The drawing shows a type of cattle that is kept by farmers in large herds to sell for meat.

Put a tick in the box next to the characteristic that farmers would want in these cattle.

Large muscles ☐

Fast runner ☐

Plentiful milk production ☐

Aggressive ☐

4 Describe how farmers could use artificial selection to produce this type of cattle.

....

....

....

Extinction

5 Read this information about the dodo bird that is shown on page 6.

> Dodos were flightless birds that only lived on one island near Africa. Sailors visited the island and often ate the birds. Rats from the ships escaped onto the island and began to eat the dodo's eggs. The dodo became extinct in the late 1600s.

The extinction of the dodo was caused by humans. Which **two** ways was this caused? Tick the correct options.

Destroying habitats ☐   Introducing foreign species ☐

Overhunting ☐   Pollution ☐

(1) What is DNA?

Genes and chromosomes

Over a hundred years ago, scientists realised that the characteristics of organisms are controlled by structures called **chromosomes**.

- Chromosomes are long chemical strands found in the nucleus of cells.
- A small section of a chromosome is called a **gene**.
- A gene controls characteristics by coding for proteins such as enzymes.

Different organisms have different numbers of chromosomes. Each human body cell has 46 chromosomes but there are only 23 in a sperm and in an egg.

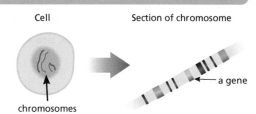

Cell   Section of chromosome

chromosomes   ← a gene

When a cell divides, the chromosomes need to be copied so that each cell gets a full set.

However, when the sex cells are made, they only get half the number of chromosomes so the full number is formed by **fertilisation**.

DNA structure

Once they knew that chromosomes contain genes, scientists tried to find out more about the structure of chromosomes. They discovered that chromosomes are made of a chemical called **DNA**.
In 1953, four scientists worked out the structure of DNA:

- **Rosalind Franklin** and **Maurice Wilkins** took photos of DNA using X-rays and showed that DNA was made up of two chains wound up in a double helix.
- **Francis Crick** and **James Watson** then built a model of a DNA molecule. They said that the chains were made of long chains of molecules containing **bases** and the bases held the two chains together. They also said that it was the order of these bases that allowed genes to code for proteins.

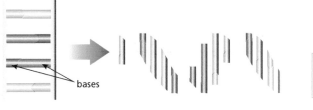

bases

Section of
uncoiled DNA

Section of DNA
forming a double helix

Sometimes the order of bases can change and this is called a **gene mutation**.

Gene technology

Since 1953, scientists have learned to 'read' the order of bases in the genes and even change them. Using or changing DNA is called **gene technology**. There are now many examples:

- **genetic fingerprints** involve reading the order of the bases to identify a person
- **genetic testing** allows doctors to look for signs of genetic diseases in the DNA
- **genetic engineering** involves putting different genes into an organism
- **gene therapy** involves replacing faulty genes to cure diseases.

What is DNA?

Genes and chromosomes

1 Complete these sentences by writing the correct words in the gaps.

The nucleus of a human cell contains many thin threads called ....

These structures contain small sections called .... , which code for

....

2 Write in each of these five green circles the number of chromosomes found in the nucleus of each human cell.

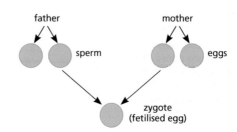

DNA structure

3 Circle the best description of the shape of a DNA molecule.

| coiled chain | double helix | single spiral | twisted fibre |

4 Put a tick in the box next to the function of DNA in living organisms.

Speeds up the rate of chemical reactions in a cell ☐

Pieces of DNA join together to make proteins ☐

Holds instructions about how to make proteins ☐

5 How did Rosalind Franklin and Maurice Wilkins help in the discovery of DNA structure?

....

....

6 Give **two** functions of the bases in a DNA molecule.

....

....

....

Gene technology

7 Doctors can now test unborn babies' DNA to look for genes coding for genetic diseases. Discuss why this can be useful for the parents but why it may also give them difficult decisions to make.

....

....

....

⦗1⦘ What are clones?

Natural animal and plant clones

A clone is a genetically identical copy of an organism. A clone can be produced naturally by **asexual reproduction**.

Examples of asexual reproduction in plants are:
- strawberry plants growing small plants from runners
- daffodil bulbs dividing into two to make new plants.

Some animals can reproduce asexually forming clones. These are usually simple animals such as starfish but human identical twins are also clones made by the embryo splitting into two.

Artificial clones

Clones can be made artificially. Gardeners often make clones by taking cuttings. They cut off a shoot and put it into soil. It can grow new roots and make a new plant.

It is harder to produce clones of animals. They can be made by dividing up embryos into separate cells. However, the first clone of an adult mammal was not made until 1996. It was a sheep called Dolly. The process used **nuclear transfer**:

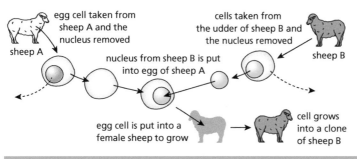

egg cell taken from sheep A and the nucleus removed

sheep A

cells taken from the udder of sheep B and the nucleus removed

sheep B

nucleus from sheep B is put into egg of sheep A

egg cell is put into a female sheep to grow

cell grows into a clone of sheep B

The sheep produced in the cloning in this diagram will be a clone of sheep B because the nucleus containing the genes comes from sheep B.

Cloning – good or bad?

Producing new plants by cloning has advantages and disadvantages compared with sexual reproduction:

Advantages	• Quicker than sexual reproduction • Only one parent plant is needed • If the parent has desired characteristics, then all offspring will show them
Disadvantage	• The offspring are all genetically identical so could all die if conditions change or a new disease appears

If an organism has been genetically engineered to produce useful proteins, then cloning can produce large numbers of this new organism.

Cloning animals is more controversial than cloning plants. Some people say that it is not **ethical** and are worried that in the future people might try to clone humans.

What are clones?

Natural animal and plant clones

1 Complete these sentences by writing the correct words in the gaps.

Asexual reproduction produces individuals that all contain the same ....

These individuals are called ....

2 Describe how a strawberry plant can produce several independent clones of itself.

....

....

....

3 Explain why human identical twins are clones, but non-identical twins are not.

....

....

....

....

Artificial clones

4 A gardener has a geranium plant that produces attractive flowers.

Describe how he could make many identical copies of this plant.

....

....

5 Dolly the sheep was produced using nuclear transfer.

What is nuclear transfer?

....

....

Cloning – good or bad?

6 Read this passage about elm trees.

> Elm trees are large trees that have grown in Britain for centuries. They often reproduce asexually by growing long horizontal roots that can grow into new trees.
>
> In ten years, 20 million elm trees in Britain were killed by a fungus that caused Dutch elm disease.

Explain why Dutch elm disease managed to kill so many elm trees in Britain.

....

....

1 What is a drug?

Why take drugs?

People take drugs for different reasons: **medical reasons** or **recreational reasons**.

	Drugs taken for medical reasons	Drugs taken for recreational reasons
What are they called?	medicines	recreational drugs
Why are they taken?	to treat illness	for the feelings they produce
How are they obtained?	legally, some with a prescription	sometimes illegally

> The same drugs may be taken as a medicine by some people and as a recreational drug by others.

Types of drugs

Drugs can be put into groups depending on the effects that they have on the body. The table shows the main groups of drugs:

Drug group	Examples	Effects on the body
painkiller	aspirin, morphine	feelings of pain are reduced or removed; pain messages are blocked in the nervous system
stimulant	caffeine, cocaine, ecstasy, nicotine	speeds up the body functions; increase in alertness, energy and brain activity
depressant	alcohol, cannabis, heroin	slows down body functions; makes a person feel relaxed or sleepy;
hallucinogen	LSD	sense of reality is distorted; makes people see things that do not exist

Side effects of drugs

Both medical and recreational drugs can have side effects:

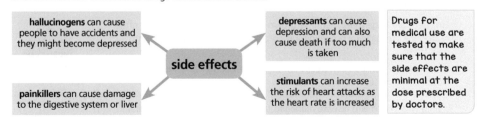

hallucinogens can cause people to have accidents and they might become depressed

painkillers can cause damage to the digestive system or liver

side effects

depressants can cause depression and can also cause death if too much is taken

stimulants can increase the risk of heart attacks as the heart rate is increased

Drugs for medical use are tested to make sure that the side effects are minimal at the dose prescribed by doctors.

Sometimes a person may become dependent on a drug and does not feel normal without it. This is called **addiction**.
- A person who is addicted will have **cravings** for the drug.
- If they stop taking the drug, they will feel ill. This is called **withdrawal effects**.

① What is a drug?

Why take drugs?

1 Why do people take recreational drugs?

_____

2 Suggest why some medicines can only be obtained with a prescription from a doctor.

_____

Types of drugs

3 Draw lines to join each drug with the group it belongs to and its effect on the body.

drug	group	effect
cannabis	hallucinogen	increases heart rate
caffeine	stimulant	slows down breathing rate
LSD	depressant	blocks pain messages
morphine	painkiller	distorts reality

Side effects of drugs

4 Give **one** possible side-effect of each of these groups of drugs:

a) depressants _____

b) stimulants _____

5 Complete these sentences by writing words in the gaps.

If a person cannot stop taking a drug without having unpleasant feelings,

then this is called an _____.

The unpleasant feelings that they suffer when they stop taking the

drug are called _____.

6 Suggest why people are more likely to have accidents when they are taking these drugs:

a) hallucinogens _____

_____

b) depressants _____

_____

How does smoking drugs affect your body?

Which drugs are smoked?

The two main substances that are smoked in the UK are **tobacco** and **cannabis**.

- Tobacco smoke contains many chemicals but the most important are **tar** and **nicotine**.
- Most people smoke tobacco in cigarettes but some smoke cigars or pipes.
- Nicotine is very addictive, which is why it is difficult to give up smoking.

- Cannabis is made from the flowers of the cannabis plant.
- When smoked, it gives off over a hundred different chemicals.
- The main substance is called **THC** but it also contains tar.

People can also breathe in tobacco or cannabis smoke from the air if they are around people who smoke. This is called **passive smoking**.

> Cannabis is known by many different names, including marijuana, weed and pot.

Effects on the body

	Tobacco	Cannabis
Pleasurable effects	• It can help people to relax.	• It can make people relaxed and calm. • It is mildly hallucinogenic.
Harmful effects	Most of the harmful effects are due to nicotine and tar: • Tar can cause infections of the lungs called **bronchitis**. It can also cause damage to the air sacs, and **lung cancer**. • Nicotine increases the heart rate and narrows blood vessels. This increases blood pressure and can lead to **heart attacks**.	The harmful effects are caused by tar and THC: • As with tobacco, the tar can cause bronchitis and lung cancer. • Long-term, THC can increase the risk of anxiety and certain mental illnesses such as schizophrenia.

> Some people eat cannabis rather than smoke it. This prevents damage to the lungs.

Legal uses of cannabis

Unlike tobacco, cannabis is not addictive but it is an illegal drug. Some people argue that cannabis should be legalised.

Doctors can prescribe cannabis for some patients. It can:
- help to relieve the muscle spasms caused by multiple sclerosis
- be used to reduce pain for cancer and HIV patients
- reduce sickness in people having chemotherapy for cancer.

RETRIEVE 1 How does smoking drugs affect your body?

Which drugs are smoked?

1 Draw lines to join the drugs to any of the chemicals that they contain.

drug

cannabis

tobacco

chemical

nicotine

tar

THC

2 How can people take in the chemicals in tobacco smoke even if they do not smoke?

Effects on the body

3 Which chemical in tobacco smoke increases blood pressure? ....

4 Write down **two** possible long-term effects of the THC in cannabis.

5 Explain why eating cannabis may cause less long-term damage to the body than smoking it.

6 The diagram shows the air sacs in the lungs of a non-smoker and a tobacco smoker.

Explain which diagram, **A** or **B**, shows the lungs of the tobacco smoker and what effect the difference in the air sacs might have on the person.

Legal uses of cannabis

7 Why is smoking cannabis not addictive but smoking tobacco is addictive?

8 Give **two** reasons why cancer patients might be prescribed cannabis.

How do alcohol and other recreational drugs affect your body?

Effects of alcohol

Alcohol is the most used drug in the UK. Although it is legal and socially acceptable, it can cause long-term side effects and even death. Alcohol is a **depressant** and therefore slows down brain function. However, different parts of the brain are slowed down at different rates, so alcohol causes a person to be less shy and increases confidence.

Possible damage from short-term use includes:
- people becoming aggressive and getting involved in fights
- balance and coordination being affected, leading to increased risks of accidents
- heart rate and breathing rate slowing down too much, leading to a coma or death.

Damage from long-term alcohol abuse includes:
- becoming addicted to alcohol (suffering **alcoholism**)
- cirrhosis of the liver, heart disease and diabetes.

> There is a lot of debate about how much alcohol is safe to drink. The government recommends that people should not regularly drink more than 14 units a week.

an average glass of wine has 2 units

half a pint of beer or cider has 1.5 units

a measure of spirit (a 'short') has 1.5 units

Effects of ecstasy and cocaine

Ecstasy and **cocaine** are both **stimulants**: they cause an increase in heart rate and body temperature. The increase in heart rate can cause a heart attack.

People use them because they make them feel happy, energetic and confident. But when the effects wear off, they often feel very depressed and anxious.

Cocaine is extremely addictive and so people will have strong cravings for more of the drug.

Effects of heroin

Heroin is a very powerful **depressant**: it makes people feel warm and relaxed.

However, it can lower heart rate and breathing rate to dangerous levels. Like cocaine, heroin is highly addictive.

> One of the main dangers of ecstasy, cocaine and heroin is that they are sold illegally, so they are seldom pure. This means that users cannot judge a safe dose and the drug may contain other dangerous chemicals.

How do alcohol and other recreational drugs affect your body?

Effects of alcohol

1. Why is drinking alcohol so popular?

....

....

2. How could drinking large amounts of alcohol in one day lead to coma or death?

....

....

3. Write down **two** long-term side effects on the body of alcohol abuse.

....

4. A person drinks these drinks in one week.

   Use the information on page 16 to calculate:

   a) how many units of alcohol the person drinks

   ....

   ....

   ....

   b) whether the person is within the government's suggested limit. Explain your answer.

   ....

   ....

   ....

3 glasses of wine

6 half pints of beer

1 measure of a spirit

Effects of ecstasy and cocaine

5. Which group of drugs do both ecstasy and cocaine belong to?

....

6. Suggest why somebody who has taken an ecstasy tablet often drinks a lot of cold water.

....

....

Effects of heroin

7. Heroin is taken by an injection or by smoking.

   Suggest the dangers to heroin addicts caused by using needles to inject heroin.

....

....

(1) How are diseases spread?

Different methods of transfer

A **disease** is something that prevents the body from working correctly. When a disease can be passed from one person to another it is called an **infectious disease**. Some diseases, such as diabetes and cancer, cannot be passed on – these are **non-infectious diseases**.

Many infectious diseases are caused by **microorganisms** (microbes). If a microbe enters your body, it will damage your cells and may release **toxins** (poisons). You start to notice symptoms of infection. Microbes are spread in different ways:

Method of spread	Details	Disease example
air	the microbes are in droplets released when somebody sneezes or coughs	influenza (flu), Covid
water/food	water and food can be contaminated by microbes	typhoid (water), salmonella (food)
faeces/urine	small amounts could contaminate objects that other people touch	ebola
blood	if needles used for injections are contaminated	HIV
animals	microbes are passed on through bites	rabies (bat and dog bites), malaria (mosquito bites)
sexual activity	this causes mixing of body fluids	HIV, chlamydia

The body's natural defences

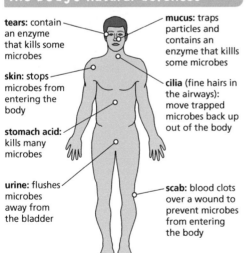

tears: contain an enzyme that kills some microbes

skin: stops microbes from entering the body

stomach acid: kills many microbes

urine: flushes microbes away from the bladder

mucus: traps particles and contains an enzyme that killls some microbes

cilia (fine hairs in the airways): move trapped microbes back up out of the body

scab: blood clots over a wound to prevent microbes from entering the body

How can we help to reduce the spread?

There are steps that we can take to lower the chance of infection:

Method of spread	Ways to reduce infection
air	sneeze/cough into tissues
water/food	improve water treatment
faeces/urine	wash hands regularly and after using the toilet
blood	use sterilised needles
animals	kill mosquitos with insecticide
sexual activity	use a condom

The mouth, nose, anus and reproductive openings are especially vulnerable to attack by microbes as they need to let substances in and out of the body.

During major epidemics, certain steps such as wearing face masks may be compulsory.

How are diseases spread?

Different methods of transfer

1 What is meant by infectious disease?

_____

_____

2 Draw straight lines to join each disease with the correct method of spread.

disease	method of spread
cholera	water
malaria	air
influenza	food
salmonella	insect bite

The body's natural defences

3 How do tears help to prevent microbes entering the body?

_____

4 How does the stomach help to prevent disease?

_____

5 The diagram shows some cells from the lining of the tubes leading to the lungs.

Explain how the mucus and cilia help to protect us from disease.

_____

_____

_____

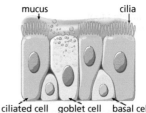

ciliated cell   goblet cell   basal cell

How can we help to reduce the spread?

6 Explain how using tissues/handkerchiefs can help to reduce the spread of influenza.

_____

_____

7 Explain how the use of insecticides helps to prevent the spread of malaria.

_____

_____

1 What are microbes?

Different types of microbes

Microorganisms (microbes) are small organisms that can only be seen using a microscope. Many infectious diseases are caused by microbes. There are three main types that can cause disease:

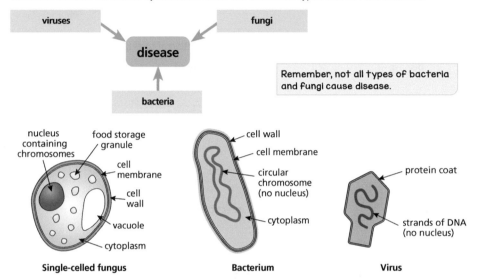

Remember, not all types of bacteria and fungi cause disease.

Single-celled fungus

nucleus containing chromosomes
food storage granule
cell membrane
cell wall
vacuole
cytoplasm

Bacterium

cell wall
cell membrane
circular chromosome (no nucleus)
cytoplasm

Virus

protein coat
strands of DNA (no nucleus)

Diseases caused by microbes

Different diseases are caused by different types of microbe:

Diseases caused by fungi	Diseases caused by bacteria	Diseases caused by viruses
athlete's foot	chlamydia	AIDS
thrush	cholera	Covid
	salmonella	ebola
	typhoid	influenza

Growing microbes

Bacteria and fungi can be grown in the laboratory. This allows scientists to study their growth and investigate the action of possible medicines.
- The microbes are grown on special plates called **Petri dishes**.
- The dishes contain a jelly called **agar**.
- The agar contains all the nutrients that the microbes need to grow.
- The plates are inoculated by spreading bacteria onto the jelly using a metal loop.
- A lid is put on the plates and they are kept warm so the microbes reproduce.

It is much more difficult to grow viruses in the lab as they only reproduce in living cells.

What are microbes?

Different types of microbes

1 Why is a microscope needed to view microbes?

_____

2 Which type of microbe contains these structures?

   a) a cell wall and a nucleus _____   **b)** a protein coat and DNA _____

3 The size of microbes is measured in units called micrometres.

The table shows the typical sizes of single-celled fungi, bacteria and viruses.

Complete the table by writing the type of microbe next to the typical size.

Typical size in micrometres	Type of microbe
0.02	
10	
2	

Diseases caused by microbes

4 Draw lines to join each disease to the type of microbe that causes it.

disease

- AIDS
- thrush
- cholera
- Covid

type of microbe

- fungus
- bacterium
- virus

Growing microbes

5 Name **two** nutrients that agar might contain to allow bacteria to grow.

_____

6 Explain why scientists wear disposable rubber gloves when inoculating Petri dishes.

_____

_____

7 Scientists want to grow bacteria that cause a human disease on a Petri dish.

Suggest what temperature they should keep the Petri dishes at. Explain your answer.

_____

1 How do antibiotics work?

Using chemicals to kill microbes

Since scientists discovered that microbes cause disease, humans have used chemicals to try to kill microbes. Different types of chemicals are used, including:

- **disinfectants**, e.g. bleach – industrially made chemicals that are used on surfaces like tables, floors and toilets to kill microbes
- **antiseptics** (sometimes taken from plants that produce antiseptic chemicals) – chemicals used on the outside of the body, often as creams or ointments, to kill microbes
- **antibiotics** – chemicals usually used inside the body by being swallowed or injected. Most are produced by fungi and they target bacteria and certain other fungi but cannot destroy viruses.

Testing antibiotics

Antibiotics help treat disease either by killing bacteria or by stopping them from reproducing. However, all antibiotics do not work on all bacteria.

Scientists need to test antibiotics on bacteria that have been grown in Petri dishes:

- a Petri dish is inoculated with bacteria
- small discs of filter paper are soaked in different antibiotics
- the discs are placed on the surface of the agar
- the discs are then kept warm.

The diagram shows the results of a test of four different antibiotics, A, B, C and D. The clear areas around the discs are where bacteria have been prevented from growing.

Petri dish

antibiotic disc

agar

lawn of bacteria

Remember that antibiotics will not destroy viruses and so cannot protect against viral diseases.

Superbugs

Since antibiotics were discovered, their use has increased. This has led to the spread of resistant strains of bacteria.

If a strain of bacteria becomes resistant to many different types of antibiotics, it can be difficult to kill. It sometimes becomes known as a **superbug**.

MRSA is a superbug that has caused major problems in some hospitals.

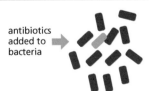

antibiotics added to bacteria

antibiotics kill off all susceptible bacteria

only a single resistant bacterium survives

bacterium multiplies to produce millions of resistant bacteria

a resistant strain of bacteria is produced

How do antibiotics work?

Using chemicals to kill microbes

1 a) What is the difference between an antiseptic and a disinfectant?

_____

_____

b) What is the difference between an antiseptic and an antibiotic?

_____

_____

2 Which type of organism makes most antibiotics?

_____

3 Explain why antibiotics cannot be used to treat Covid.

_____

Testing antibiotics

4 Write down **two** ways that antibiotics may affect bacteria.

_____

5 Look at the diagram of the Petri dish on page 22.

Which antibiotic, A, B, C or D, would be best for treating a disease caused by this bacterium?

Explain your answer.

_____

Superbugs

6 What is a superbug?

_____

7 Look at the graph. It shows the percentage of one type of bacteria in different countries that are resistant to many antibiotics.

It also shows antibiotic use in each country.

a) Which country uses most antibiotics?

_____

b) What pattern is shown between antibiotic use and percentage resistance of bacteria?

_____

_____

_____

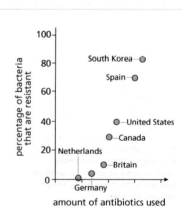

ORGANISE

1 How do vaccinations work?

Immunity and memory cells

If a microbe gets through a person's natural defences and enters the body, then there are other defences, one of which is **white blood cells**.

White blood cells destroy microbes in two main ways:

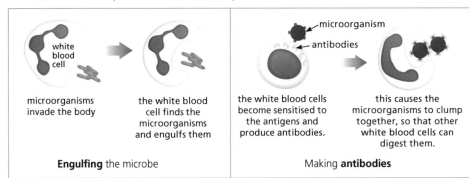

microorganisms invade the body	the white blood cell finds the microorganisms and engulfs them

Engulfing the microbe

the white blood cells become sensitised to the antigens and produce antibodies.

this causes the microorganisms to clump together, so that other white blood cells can digest them.

Making **antibodies**

When the person recovers from the disease, some white blood cells become **memory cells**. This means that if the microbes return, the memory cells can produce antibodies quickly, which prevents the person from getting ill again. This is called **immunity**.

Vaccinations

A vaccination gives the body some immunity to a disease.

a **vaccine** containing a weakened or dead disease-causing microbe is injected into the body		white blood cells make antibodies and memory cells against the microbe		if the person gets infected by the live microbe, the memory cells stop the person getting ill

Some microbes, like the viruses that cause influenza and Covid, change quite regularly. This means that scientists must keep changing the vaccine.

Problems with vaccinations

All medicines, including vaccinations, can have side effects. Usually, these are not very serious and include things like:
- headaches
- mild fever
- pain at the site of injection.

The use of vaccinations is all about balancing risks and gains. Although vaccinations may have caused occasional serious side effects, they have saved millions of lives.

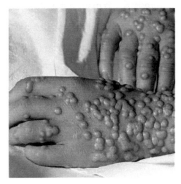

Smallpox used to kill millions of people but in 1978 it had disappeared, due to vaccination.

24

How do vaccinations work?

Immunity and memory cells

1 Complete these sentences about how the body destroys microbes by filling in the gaps.

If a microbe gets through the body's barriers it is attacked by .... blood cells.

These cells may surround the microbe and .... it.

They may also produce molecules called .... that will stick the microbes together.

2 **a)** How is a memory cell produced?

....

....

b) Explain how a memory cell gives us immunity.

....

....

....

Vaccinations

3 What does a vaccine contain?

....

4 Why does a new influenza vaccination need to be made every year?

....

....

....

5 Sometimes a person develops mild symptoms of the disease after having a vaccination.

Suggest why this is.

....

....

Problems with vaccinations

6 Vaccines are carefully tested before they are offered to the whole population.

Give reasons why.

....

....

....

7 What was the first disease to be eliminated by vaccination?

....

(2) Do all metals react the same?

Metals and the reactivity series

Metals are found on the left and centre of the **Periodic Table**. **Alloys** are **mixtures** that are made of mainly metals to create stronger metals.

The **reactivity series** is a list of metals from most reactive to least reactive. This order is made from careful observation of the reaction of metals with oxygen, water and acids.

Hydrogen and carbon are often put in the reactivity series for a comparison:
* only the metals above hydrogen in the reactivity series react with **acids**
* all metals below carbon in the reactivity series can be **extracted** from their ore using carbon.

most reactive	K	potassium
	Na	sodium
	Ca	calcium
	Mg	magnesium
	Al	aluminium
	C	carbon
	Zn	zinc
	Fe	iron
	Sn	tin
	Pb	lead
	H	hydrogen
	Cu	copper
	Ag	silver
least reactive	Au	gold
	Pt	platinum

> When a metal reacts with an acid, a metal salt and hydrogen gas is made. Hydrogen can be collected and tested: hydrogen gas causes a squeaky pop when a lighted splint is put into it.

Displacement reactions

In a **displacement reaction**, a more reactive element will take the place of a less reactive element from its compound. This is a **chemical change**.

For example, iron is more reactive than copper. So, when an iron nail is put into a blue solution of copper sulfate, the iron displaces the copper from its compound. This forms a green solution of iron sulfate and the rose-coloured copper metal forms on the surface of the nail.

The reactivity series can be used to predict if a displacement reaction will happen:
* Look at the reactivity series and find the two metals that are involved in the reaction.
* The metal that is highest in the reactivity series is the one that will be in the compound.
* So, if the more reactive metal is in a compound to start with, no reaction will happen.

Single displacement reaction

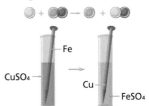

Fe

CuSO₄

Cu

FeSO₄

$$Fe + CuSO_4 \rightarrow Cu + FeSO_4$$

Thermal decomposition

Thermal decomposition is a chemical change where heat is used to break down a substance.

Some metal carbonates can undergo thermal decomposition to make a metal oxide and carbon dioxide.

For example, copper carbonate can be heated strongly with a Bunsen burner to make copper oxide and carbon dioxide gas. The gas can be blown through limewater which will go from colourless to cloudy, showing that carbon dioxide was formed.

Decomposition reaction

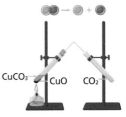

CuCO₃

CuO

CO₂

$$CuCO_3 \rightarrow CuO + CO_2$$

② Do all metals react the same?

Metals and the reactivity series

1 Where are the metals found on the Periodic Table?

....

2 What is an alloy?

....

3 **a)** What is the reactivity series?

....

b) Why are carbon and hydrogen added to the reactivity series?

....

c) Predict whether tin (Sn) will react with hydrochloric acid. Explain your answer.

....

....

Displacement reactions

4 Decide whether each of the following statements is **true** or **false** and put a tick in the correct column.

	True	False
a) Displacement reactions are chemical changes.		
b) A less reactive element will take the place of a more reactive element in its compound.		
c) More reactive elements are found at the top of the reactivity series.		
d) Hydrogen gas is made in a metal displacement reaction.		
e) A displacement reaction would happen between copper sulfate solution and magnesium.		

Thermal decomposition

5 **a)** Complete the word equation.

.... → calcium oxide + carbon dioxide

b) Complete the word equation.

lead carbonate → .... + ...

How are metals extracted from the Earth?

Metals in nature

Native metals like gold (Au) and platinum (Pt) are metals that are found uncombined (pure) in nature. But most metals are so reactive that they are found in compounds called **minerals**, for example, copper.

Copper ore – malachite $CuCO_3(OH)_2$ Copper metal – Cu

Rocks contain minerals, and if there is enough to make it financially worth extracting, the rock is called an **ore**. The **yield** is calculated to show what percentage of the rock is the metal.

$$yield = \frac{actual\ mass\ produced}{theoretical\ mass\ produced} \times 100$$

Native metals were the first metals that were used by humans. As technology developed, metals could be extracted from *minerals and more metals were discovered.*

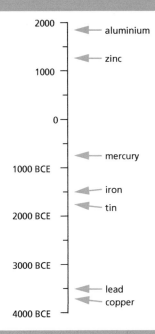

Metal extraction

Mining is the method used to get ores. The ores are then processed to extract pure metals.

However, mining can have a negative impact. For example:
- deep mining can cause **subsidence**, which can make the ground unstable and cave in
- waste rock and materials can leach and cause toxic chemicals to pollute soils and water
- carbon extraction methods produce greenhouse gases, which are linked to **climate change**
- acidic gases are produced during the extraction process, which can cause **acid rain**
- visual and noise pollution from the mine affects local people.

The negative impact of a mine can be reduced with careful planning. Gases can be treated and neutralised as well as toxic material being specially stored to prevent pollution. Old mines can be reclaimed and made into nature reserves.

Recycling

Metals are a **finite** (non-renewable) resource extracted from the Earth's crust, and they will run out. Therefore, **recycling** is important so there is enough metal available in the future. Recycling uses less energy than extracting metals from rocks and produces fewer **greenhouse gases**.

How are metals extracted from the Earth?

Metals in nature

1 Draw lines to match the key term on the left to the correct definition on the right.

key term	definition
mineral	more than one type of atom chemically joined
ore	a metal compound found in nature
compound	a rock where the percentage of metal is high enough that it is financially worth extracting

2 A 100 kg sample of malachite rock made 2 kg of pure copper. Calculate the percentage yield of pure copper.

3 What is a native metal?

Metal extraction

4 Decide whether each of the following statements is **true** or **false** by putting a tick in the correct column.

	True	False
a) Mining is how minerals are processed to get pure metals.		
b) Leaching can be prevented by trapping the waste.		
c) Subsidence is caused by deep mines.		
d) Carbon extraction methods can lead to climate change.		
e) There is no noise or visual pollution from a mine.		

Recycling

5 **a)** Explain why recycling is important in terms of energy.

b) Explain why recycling is important in terms of non-renewable (finite) resources.

② How is carbon used to extract metals?

Reduction using carbon

Reduction is a chemical reaction where oxygen is removed from a substance. All metals below carbon in the reactivity series can be extracted from their oxides using carbon; by heating the mixture of metal oxide and coke (an impure form of carbon) to form the metal and carbon dioxide gas.

Iron	Powdered coke (impure carbon), hematite (iron ore) and limestone are crushed and added to the **blast furnace**. Molten iron is tapped from the bottom of the furnace.	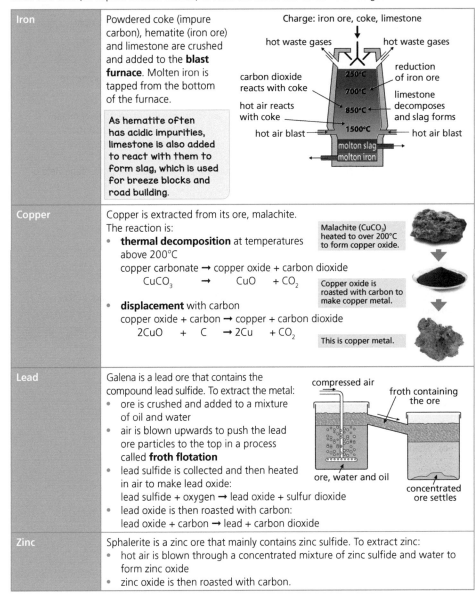 Charge: iron ore, coke, limestone
	As hematite often has acidic impurities, limestone is also added to react with them to form slag, which is used for breeze blocks and road building.	
Copper	Copper is extracted from its ore, malachite. The reaction is: • **thermal decomposition** at temperatures above 200°C copper carbonate → copper oxide + carbon dioxide $CuCO_3 \rightarrow CuO + CO_2$ • **displacement** with carbon copper oxide + carbon → copper + carbon dioxide $2CuO + C \rightarrow 2Cu + CO_2$	Malachite ($CuCO_3$) heated to over 200°C to form copper oxide. Copper oxide is roasted with carbon to make copper metal. This is copper metal.
Lead	Galena is a lead ore that contains the compound lead sulfide. To extract the metal: • ore is crushed and added to a mixture of oil and water • air is blown upwards to push the lead ore particles to the top in a process called **froth flotation** • lead sulfide is collected and then heated in air to make lead oxide: lead sulfide + oxygen → lead oxide + sulfur dioxide • lead oxide is then roasted with carbon: lead oxide + carbon → lead + carbon dioxide	compressed air froth containing the ore ore, water and oil concentrated ore settles
Zinc	Sphalerite is a zinc ore that mainly contains zinc sulfide. To extract zinc: • hot air is blown through a concentrated mixture of zinc sulfide and water to form zinc oxide • zinc oxide is then roasted with carbon.	

Blast furnace diagram labels: hot waste gases — hot waste gases; reduction of iron ore; 250°C; carbon dioxide reacts with coke; 700°C; limestone decomposes and slag forms; hot air reacts with coke; 850°C; hot air blast; 1500°C; hot air blast; molton slag; molton iron

② How is carbon used to extract metals?

Reduction using carbon

1 a) What is a reduction reaction?

_____

b) Which gas is always produced when metals are reduced using carbon?

Tick the correct option.

hydrogen ☐

carbon dioxide ☐

oxygen ☐

methane ☐

2 What name is given to the raw material containing carbon that is used in the blast furnace?

_____

3 What is the name of iron ore?

_____

4 Decide whether each of the following statements is **true** or **false** by putting a tick in the correct column.

	True	False
a) Extracting copper from malachite involves thermal decomposition and displacement.		
b) Copper can displace carbon from its compound.		
c) Galena is a copper ore.		
d) Malachite mainly contains the compound, copper oxide.		
e) Copper carbonate, copper oxide and copper are all green compounds.		

5 What is the name of lead ore?

_____

6 What compound containing zinc is found in sphalerite?

_____

How can energy be used to classify a reaction?

Chemical reactions

In a **chemical change** a new substance is made. The reaction can be modelled in three steps:

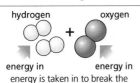

hydrogen   oxygen

energy in   energy in
energy is taken in to break the
bonds in the **reactants**

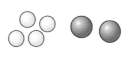

the individual atoms rearrange

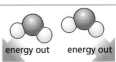

energy out   energy out

new bonds are made to form the
products and energy is released.

Most chemical reactions need energy to get started. This is called the **activation energy**.

Exothermic and endothermic changes

In an **exothermic change**, energy is released from the reaction to the surroundings. This causes a temperature rise.

Examples include:
- metal and acid reactions
- freezing water into ice
- burning in a campfire

In an exothermic reaction, more energy is released when the product bonds form, than the amount needed to break the reactant bonds.

In an **endothermic change**, energy is taken in from the surroundings. This causes a temperature drop.

Examples include:
- dissolving salt in water
- baking bread
- cooking an egg
- photosynthesis
- water evaporation

In an endothermic reaction, less energy is released when the product bonds form, than the amount needed to break the reactant bonds.

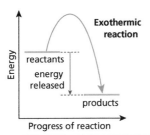

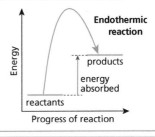

Endothermic chemical changes are rare. But real-life examples include thermal decomposition of metal carbonates and the neutralisation of citric acid by bicarbonate of soda in a sherbet sweet.

Monitoring reactions

Use a thermometer to monitor any temperature change:
- If the temperature increases = exothermic change
- If the temperatute decreases = endothermic change

exothermic reaction in which heat is given out

endothermic reaction in which heat is taken in

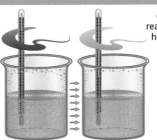

How can energy be used to classify a reaction?

Chemical reactions

1 Decide whether each of the following statements is **true** or **false** by putting a tick in the correct column.

	True	False
a) Chemical changes always make a new substance.		
b) Energy is needed to make bonds.		
c) Energy is released when products are made.		
d) In a chemical reaction, atoms rearrange.		
e) Energy is absorbed to form atoms from the reactants.		

Exothermic and endothermic changes

2 **a)** What is an exothermic change?

....

b) Give an example of a physical change that is exothermic.

....

3 **a)** What is an endothermic change?

....

b) Give an example of a chemical change that is endothermic.

....

4 Label each of these diagrams as **exothermic** or **endothermic**.

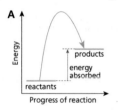

A — Energy / Progress of reaction; reactants, products, energy absorbed

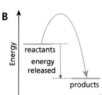

B — Energy / Progress of reaction; reactants, energy released, products

Monitoring reactions

5 Describe how you can monitor a change and classify it as exothermic or endothermic.

....

....

....

....

(2) What are catalysts?

Catalysts

Catalysts are substances that are added to a chemical reaction to change the **rate of reaction** (speed). The rate of reaction is a measure of how quickly a product is made or a reactant is used up.

Most catalysts allow the reaction to happen with less **activation energy** and so, the reaction happens faster.

Catalysts are:
- specific to one reaction
- not used up in the reaction
- unchanged at the end of the reaction
- written on the arrow of an equation as it is not a **reactant** or a **product**.

Catalysts are used in industry to make the production of substances more profitable by:
- reducing the temperature and therefore the energy needed for the reaction
- reducing the amount of time it takes to make the products
- increasing the **yield** of a reaction.

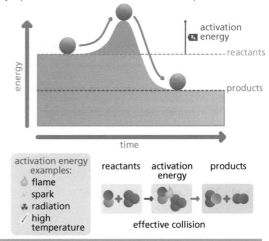

activation energy examples:
- 🜄 flame
- 🗲 spark
- ☢ radiation
- 🌡 high temperature

Catalytic converters

Car exhaust pipes are often fitted with **catalytic converters** to remove harmful gases. The substances that are released by the catalytic converter are already found naturally in the air.

The **word equations** for the reactions in a catalytic converter are:
- nitrogen oxide → nitrogen + oxygen
- carbon monoxide + oxygen → carbon dioxide
- hydrocarbon + oxygen → water + carbon dioxide

harmful exhaust gases (nitrogen oxides, carbon monoxide, hydrocarbons) enter

platinum and rhodium lining acts as a catalyst

nitrogen oxides are converted to nitrogen

carbon monoxide is converted to carbon dioxide

hydrocarbons react to form carbon dioxide and water

less harmful gases released into air

Enzymes

Enzymes are **biological catalysts** that change the speed of reactions in organisms (living things). The enzyme works with a reactant molecule (**substrate**) fitting into the enzyme like a **lock and key**.

Without enzymes, the chemical reactions in human body cells would be too slow to keep us alive.

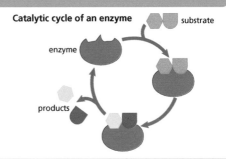

Catalytic cycle of an enzyme   substrate

enzyme

products

In digestion, enzymes break down large insoluble food molecules into small soluble food molecules and release them. The enzyme is unchanged at the end of the reaction and is then free to work again.

2 What are catalysts?

Catalysts

1 Draw lines to match the key term on the left to the correct definition on the right.

key term

definition

rate of reaction

a substance that changes the speed of a chemical reaction without being used up itself

catalyst

the minimum amount of energy to start a chemical reaction

activation energy

a measure of how quickly a product is made or a reactant is used up

2 If 10g of catalyst was added to a reaction, what mass of catalyst would be collected at the end?

3 Where would you write the name of the catalyst in a word equation? Tick the correct answer.

on the left of the arrow ☐

over the arrow ☐

on the right of the arrow ☐

4 Why are catalysts widely used in industry?

5 How does using a catalyst save energy?

Catalytic converters

6 Describe the function of a catalytic converter.

7 Complete the word equation for the oxidation of a hydrocarbon in a catalytic converter.

hydrocarbon + _____ → water + _____

Enzymes

8 **a)** What is an enzyme?

b) Why are enzymes important?

② What are ceramics?

Ceramics and their uses

A **ceramic** is an **inorganic** (not carbon-based), non-metallic solid. It is prepared by the action of heat followed by cooling.

> Clay and sand were important ingredients in early ceramics but modern ceramics are now based on oxides like aluminium oxide. The mix is carefully chosen to give the exact properties that are wanted in the final ceramic.

Most ceramics are:
- **durable** – hard and resistant to wear
- low density – light for their size
- **brittle** – they can break easily if a force is applied and cannot be drawn into wires
- thermal **insulators** – they keep heat in
- electrical insulators – they do not allow electric current to pass through
- non-magnetic
- chemically stable – they do not break down in air and are non-toxic.

There are three categories of ceramics:
- **refractory** – retain their strength at high temperatures, and resist corrosion and chemical attack; they are used in furnaces
- **structural** – hard, strong and do not react with the environment; they can be used for tiles, glass and brick
- **whiteware** – stable, durable and non-toxic and can be made into any shape and decorated; they can be used for cooking pots and tableware.

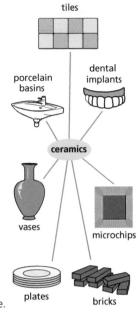

tiles

porcelain basins

dental implants

ceramics

vases

microchips

plates

bricks

Structure of ceramics

There are two main types of ceramic structure:

crystalline	amorphous
usually made from one or more varieties of a metal oxide	(meaning 'without shape') – glass-based ceramics come into this category. ●oxygen ●silicon

Problems with ceramics

There are some drawbacks of using ceramics:
- Clay and other raw materials must be mined from the Earth's crust to make them. This changes the ecosystem of the area, can cause pollution and releases greenhouse gases.
- Making ceramics needs a number of stages and it is difficult to get the correct conditions throughout the manufacture. This means the end products may have defects, so they are not suitable for their function, causing waste.
- Very high temperatures are needed to make ceramics. This uses a lot of energy and is a costly process.

② What are ceramics?

Ceramics and their uses

1 Decide whether each of the following statements is **true** or **false** by putting a tick in the correct column.

	True	False
a) Ceramics are organic, non-metal solids.		
b) Ceramics are made through heating and cooling.		
c) Most ceramics are brittle.		
d) Ceramics are toxic.		
e) All permanent magnets are made from ceramics.		

2 Draw lines to match the type of ceramic on the left to its use on the right.

ceramic

use

refractory

used to make a roofing material

structural

used to make pots to cook food in and then put in the fridge to keep

whiteware

used as a heat shield on the outside of space vehicles

Structure of ceramics

3 What substance is usually found in crystalline ceramics?

4 What ceramic category is glass?

Problems with ceramics

5 Why is the manufacturing of ceramics difficult?

6 Why is it important not to drop ceramics?

② What are polymers?

Polymers

A **polymer** is a substance made of long chains of repeating chemical units – the repeating molecule is called a **monomer**.

Most polymers are:
- strong, because of the number of chemical bonds
- solids at room temperature because of the strength of the forces between the polymer molecules
- insulators as they do not let electricity or heat flow easily through them
- chemically stable, which makes them non-toxic but also non-biodegradable
- flexible and elastic as the long polymer chains are tangled up in their natural state and they straighten to long lengths when a force is applied.

monomers

polymerisation

polymer

Natural polymers

There are many natural polymers that are found in organisms. Here are some:
- **Starch** – 1000 glucose molecules join up to make one polymer molecule of starch.

> Glucose is made by plants in photosynthesis. The excess glucose is stored in the plant as starch because it is insoluble in cold water whereas glucose can dissolve. When the plant needs the glucose, carbohydrase (an enzyme) breaks down the starch molecule back into glucose.

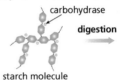

carbohydrase

digestion

starch molecule   sugar molecule

- **Protein** – made from amino acid monomers. It is used in the body to make muscle, hormones, enzymes and haemoglobin. The arrangement of the polymer gives the structure, which usually has a particular shape so that it can complete functions in organisms.
- **Latex** (**rubber**) – a natural polymer made from the sap of the rubber tree.
- **Deoxyribonucleic acid (DNA)** – the store of genetic information in cells.
- **Cellulose** – makes up plant cell walls. It is strong, tough and insoluble, which allows the plant cell to keep its shape. It can also be used to make fibres.

Synthetic polymers

Synthetic polymers are made by scientists and engineers. They usually use crude oil as their raw material and contain mainly hydrogen and carbon atoms.

Monomers are carefully selected and heated under great pressure with catalysts until the desired polymer is made. One of the first synthetic polymers to be made was polyethene, formed by many ethene monomers joining together to make a very long polymer chain. It is used to make plastic bags, plastic containers, cling film and plastic milk bottles.

By understanding how the structure of the polymer affects the properties, it is possible to design polymers for a specific function:
- Length of polymer chains – the longer the polymer chains, the higher the melting and boiling point and the more viscous (thick) the liquid polymer will be.
- **Cross links** – small amounts of other elements are added into the polymer, which can add strength and allow the polymer to form a gel.
- Branching – density, strength and rigidity of the polymer is increased when there is less branching.

ethene

polythene

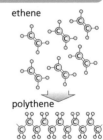

polymer structure

linear   branched   cross-linked

② What are polymers?

Polymers

1 What is a polymer?

....

Natural polymers

2 What is the name of the monomer that makes up starch?

....

3 What is the name of the polymer made from amino acids?

....

Synthetic polymers

4 Describe how synthetic polymers are made.

....

....

5 Draw lines to match the property of the polymer on the left to how the structure causes it.

property

high melting and boiling point

density

ability to form a gel

how structure causes it

how straight or branched the polymer chain is

presence of cross-links

strength of forces between the polymer chains

6 Write down the letter of the diagram that represents each polymer structure.

a) Linear ☐

b) Cross-linked ☐

c) Branched ☐

A   B   C

② What are composites?

Composites

A **composite** is a material made from two or more substances that have been mixed together but are still recognisable. Each substance will have different properties and they are not chemically joined in the composite.

Carbon-fibre is a composite that is heat-resistant as well as having high strength. It is made from:
- **matrix** – mainly a plastic
- **reinforcement** – a small amount of carbon fibre that is spread out in the plastic.

Composites have more desirable properties than the separate substances. Usually they are more **durable** and stronger.

Natural composites

Wood is a natural composite made of **cellulose** and **lignin**. The strong and tough lignin acts like a glue, binding the fibres of cellulose together.

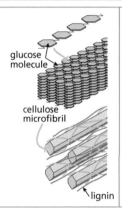

glucose molecule

cellulose microfibril

lignin

Bone is a natural composite made from **collagen** and calcium phosphate. Collagen is a soft, flexible **protein** reinforced by the mineral to make it stronger, so the bone is strong but also slightly flexible and not brittle.

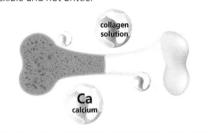

collagen solution

Ca
calcium

Synthetic composites

Synthetic composites are designed by scientists and made by engineers. They include:
- **fibreglass** – short glass fibres with a polyester matrix, which results in a strong and lightweight material that is cheap and easily moulded and is used to make boats and insulation
- **cermet** – a ceramic matrix often made of titanium carbide with metal particles added, which makes a material resistant to high temperature that may conduct electricity. It is used to make hip replacements and machine tools.

Concrete

Concrete was used as a building material in 6500 BCE and it is still used today. It is made from:
- matrix of cement made from heating limestone and clay to 700°C in a kiln
- reinforcements of aggregate (gravel and sand).

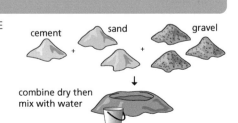

cement + sand + gravel

combine dry then mix with water

Ancient Egyptians used synthetic composites: their building bricks were a mixture of mud and straw. The straw was not chemically combined to the mud, but added strength and durability.

② What are composites?

Composites

1 Why are composites sometimes used instead of pure substances?

....

2 Draw lines to match the key term on the left to the correct definition on the right.

key term	definition
composite	the main material that makes up a composite
matrix	the material spread out within the composite
reinforcement	a material made from two or more substances that have been mixed together but are still recognisable

Natural composites

3 What is the matrix in wood?

....

4 What is the reinforcement in bone?

....

Synthetic composites

5 Which of the following statements about synthetic composites is **true**? Tick the correct option.

Synthetic composites are found in the natural world. ☐

Fibreglass has glass as the matrix. ☐

Fibreglass is strong and dense. ☐

Cermet always contains titanium carbide. ☐

Cermet is used to make hip replacements. ☐

Concrete

6 What is concrete made from?

....

(2) What is the atmosphere?

Development of the atmosphere

The **atmosphere** is the envelope of gas that surrounds the planet. The atmosphere is made of a mixture of gases called **air**.

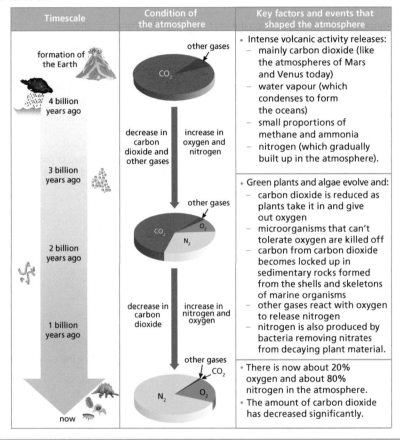

Timescale	Condition of the atmosphere	Key factors and events that shaped the atmosphere
formation of the Earth / 4 billion years ago	other gases / CO_2	• Intense volcanic activity releases: – mainly carbon dioxide (like the atmospheres of Mars and Venus today) – water vapour (which condenses to form the oceans) – small proportions of methane and ammonia – nitrogen (which gradually built up in the atmosphere).
3 billion years ago	decrease in carbon dioxide and other gases / increase in oxygen and nitrogen other gases / CO_2 / O_2 / N_2	• Green plants and algae evolve and: – carbon dioxide is reduced as plants take it in and give out oxygen – microorganisms that can't tolerate oxygen are killed off – carbon from carbon dioxide becomes locked up in sedimentary rocks formed from the shells and skeletons of marine organisms – other gases react with oxygen to release nitrogen – nitrogen is also produced by bacteria removing nitrates from decaying plant material.
2 billion years ago		
1 billion years ago	decrease in carbon dioxide / increase in nitrogen and oxygen other gases / CO_2 / N_2 / O_2	• There is now about 20% oxygen and about 80% nitrogen in the atmosphere. • The amount of carbon dioxide has decreased significantly.
now		

Air pollution

Air pollution is the release of harmful substances into the air. Air pollution can be:
• natural, e.g. caused by forest fires, volcanic eruptions, wind erosion, pollen dispersal and natural radioactivity
• man-made, e.g. caused by burning of fuels, emissions from factories, homes and farms.

> Scientists play an important role in researching greener alternatives to burning fossil fuels, as well as how to remove substances before they pollute the air.

The effects of air pollution include:
• **climate change** as greenhouse gases trap extra heat energy in the atmosphere
• **acid rain** as the acidic gases mix with water and cause rain that damages ecosystems
• **smog**, which is a mixture of smoke and fog that can cause respiratory problems
• the **ozone hole** that has been caused by the use of CFCs and is increasing cases of skin cancer and cataracts.

② What is the atmosphere?

Development of the atmosphere

1 Approximately how old is the Earth?

....

2 **a)** What was the main gas in the early atmosphere?

....

b) What process caused oxygen to be added to our atmosphere?

....

3 What are the **two** main gases in dry air?

....

4 Which of the following statements about the current atmosphere is correct?

Tick the correct option.

There is approximately 20% oxygen and 80% nitrogen in the atmosphere. ☐

There is approximately 20% nitrogen and 80% oxygen in the atmosphere. ☐

There is approximately 20% oxygen and 80% carbon dioxide in the atmosphere. ☐

There is approximately 20% carbon dioxide and 80% oxygen in the atmosphere. ☐

Air pollution

5 What is air pollution?

....

....

6 Decide whether each of the following statements is **true** or **false** by putting a tick in the correct column.

	True	False
a) Air pollution can only be man-made.		
b) Climate change is caused by greenhouse gases being released into the atmosphere.		
c) Acid rain causes changes in ecosystems.		
d) Carbon dioxide pollution causes the ozone hole.		
e) Smog can cause climate change.		

② What is climate change?

The greenhouse effect

Greenhouse gases like water (H_2O) and carbon dioxide (CO_2) that are naturally found in our atmosphere cause a warming effect. But humans are adding more greenhouse gases to the atmosphere and changing the natural balance.

The greenhouse effect is:
- natural
- slow and relatively constant
- needed to keep temperatures high enough to support life as we know it.

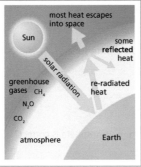

The human enhanced greenhouse effect (global warming) is:
- man-made
- fast (since the late 1800s)
- possibly able to cause an extinction level event.

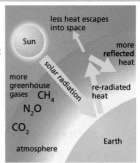

An increase of carbon dioxide in the atmosphere may result in longer growing seasons in temperate regions and faster growth for some crops. This is because the rate of photosynthesis is increased as the concentration of carbon dioxide increases.

The human-enhanced greenhouse effect leads to **climate change** and causes:
- polar ice sheets to melt
- sea levels to rise, which will flood low-lying land and cause habitat loss
- weather patterns to change, which leads to food shortage, drought and desertification
- low-lying areas of the world to become submerged and habitat loss for many species
- an increase in severe weather events
- tropical disease to affect more parts of the world.

To reduce the impact of the human-enhanced greenhouse effect we need to:
- reduce greenhouse gas emissions by reducing use of fossil fuels and using more renewable sources of energy
- reduce the greenhouse gases already in the atmosphere by increasing the number of photosynthesising plants and algae, and carbon capture with storage.

The carbon cycle and carbon footprint

Carbon atoms are converted into many different compounds in organisms and chemical reactions on our planet. The **carbon cycle** describes the relationships.

A **carbon footprint** is a measure of the impact that all our activities have on the environment. It calculates the total amount of greenhouse gases that we are expected to produce, measured in units of carbon dioxide.

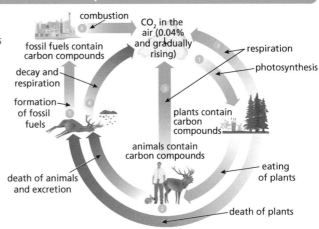

② What is climate change?

The greenhouse effect

1 Draw lines to match the key term on the left to the correct definition on the right.

key term

definition

greenhouse gas

greenhouse effect

global warming

the increase in average world temperatures

the natural trapping of solar radiation to keep average world temperatures stable

a gas that traps solar radiation in the atmosphere

2 What causes climate change?

_____

3 Suggest **two** ways in which the effect of the human-enhanced greenhouse effect can be reduced.

_____

_____

_____

_____

The carbon cycle and carbon footprint

4 Decide whether each of the following statements is **true** or **false** by putting a tick in the correct column.

	True	False
a) Respiration releases carbon dioxide into the atmosphere.		
b) Fossil fuels trap carbon for hundreds of years.		
c) Photosynthesis increases the level of carbon dioxide in the atmosphere.		
d) Only animals respire.		
e) Combustion of fossil fuels can lead to climate change.		

5 What are the units of carbon footprint?

_____

How can we protect the Earth's resources?

Resources

The Earth provides **natural resources** that help humans live. Many raw materials are taken from the Earth by **quarrying** and **mining**, which can have environmental impacts.

Animal resources

Crude oil

Forest resources

Precious metals, minerals, rocks

Water resources

Land resources

Wind power and solar energy

Natural gas

Resources that are used faster than the Earth can replace them are **non-renewable** or **finite resources**. Resources that will never run out, or are being used at a slower rate than they can be replaced, are **renewable resources**.	**Renewable energy** 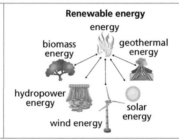	**Non-renewable energy** 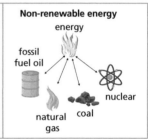

Sustainability

Sustainability is about living today as we want to, but making sure there are enough resources for future generations to live as they want to as well. This means changing how we live now by moving away from using and disposing in order to reduce, reuse and **recycle**.

Recycling

Recycling is taking products at the end of their useful life, breaking them down into their separate resources then cleaning them and shaping them into new products. Metals, glass and some plastics are easily recycled by melting and then recasting or reforming into different products.

Recycling uses less energy, makes less pollution, reduces carbon footprint and is quicker than using materials for the first time.

Down-cycling is where the recycled material is made into something that cannot then go on to be recycled itself. An example is PET drinks bottles, which are recycled into clothing fibres, but the clothing fibres cannot then be recycled.

Plastic products recycling process

How can we protect the Earth's resources?

Resources

1. Decide whether each of the following resources is **renewable** or **non-renewable** by putting a tick in the correct column.

	Renewable	Non-renewable
a) Hematite (iron ore)		
b) Solar power		
c) Fossil fuels		
d) Nuclear fuel		
e) Wood		

2. Name **two** ways in which raw materials are taken from the Earth.

Sustainability

3. What is meant by sustainability?

4. What are the **three** main ways to reduce waste?

Recycling

5. Explain how metals are recycled.

6. Explain what is meant by down-cycling.

7. Why is recycling important?

2 What is the Earth made from?

Structure of the Earth

The Earth is made up of a number of layers:
- **lithosphere** – solid outside of the Earth, made of the crust split into large sections called **plates** and the semi-liquid top part of the **mantle**
- **mantle** – convection currents cause liquid rock containing oxides of magnesium, iron and silicon to move
- **core** – made from iron and nickel.

It is difficult to study the structure of the Earth directly because the crust is too thick to drill right through. So instead, scientists study how waves made by earthquakes and explosions travel through the Earth.

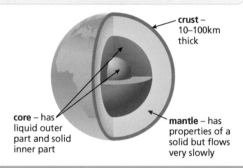

crust – 10–100km thick

core – has liquid outer part and solid inner part

mantle – has properties of a solid but flows very slowly

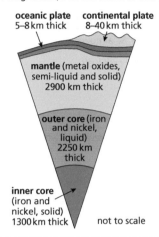

oceanic plate 5–8 km thick   continental plate 8–40 km thick

mantle (metal oxides, semi-liquid and solid) 2900 km thick

outer core (iron and nickel, liquid) 2250 km thick

inner core (iron and nickel, solid) 1300 km thick   not to scale

Earth's crust

The Earth's crust is split into about 20 large pieces known as plates. The plates slowly move and cause the land masses to change position in a process called **continental drift**.

Pangaea
(Permian 250 million years ago)

Laurasia and Gondwana
(Triassic 200 million years ago)

Present
(Quarternary)

Pangaea

Tethys Ocean

Laurasia

Gondwana

Tethys Ocean

Arctic Ocean

North America

Atlantic Ocean

Pacific Ocean

South America

Eurasia

Africa

Pacific Ocean

Indian Ocean

Australia

Antarctica

Each plate can be made from one of two types of crust:
- oceanic crust – made of basalt and is dense and thin
- continental crust – made from granite and is less dense.

Plate boundaries are where the plates meet. This is where earthquakes and volcanoes are often found.

←ocean

←oceanic crust   oceanic crust→

convection currents in the mantle   hot molten rock   convection currents

Plate boundaries

subduction

spreading

lateral sliding

② What is the Earth made from?

Structure of the Earth

1 Draw lines to match each layer of the Earth on the left to the correct description on the right.

crust	the centre is solid and the outside is liquid
mantle	solid material made of two different densities
core	liquid and semi-liquid rock

2 What is the lithosphere made from?

....

3 Draw lines to match each layer of the Earth on the left to the correct composition on the right.

crust	metal and silica oxides
mantle	iron and nickel
core	basalt and granite

4 Use the following words to label the diagram of the Earth.

inner core   outer core   crust   mantle

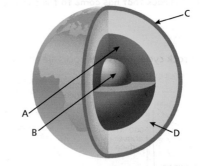

A: ....

B: ....

C: ....

D: ....

Earth's crust

5 Which type of the Earth's crust is the densest?

....

6 How many plates are there in the crust of the Earth? ....

7 What is continental drift?

....

....

② What is the rock cycle?

Rocks

Rocks are the solid mineral material that makes up the crust of the Earth. There are three groups of rocks: sedimentary rocks, igneous rocks and metamorphic rocks.

Sedimentary rocks have layers, **grains** and **fossils**, e.g. limestone and sandstone.	**Igneous rocks** have **crystals** and no fossils, e.g. granite and basalt.	**Metamorphic rocks** often have crystals and layers that are squashed, e.g. marble and slate.
		**A** Extreme compressional forces **B** Crushing and grinding of rocks **C** Interaction with a high-temperature fluid **D** Around intrusive igneous rocks
A Erosion – particles carried away by wind or water **B Deposition** – loosely packed sediments **C Compaction** – closely packed sediments **D Cementation** – tightly packed sediments	extrusive (volcanic) igneous rocks intrusive igneous rocks	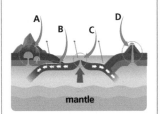 mantle

Magma is liquid rock, and when it cools and solidifies, it forms intrusive igneous rocks. Lava is molten rock that has come to the surface and when it cools it forms extrusive igneous rocks.

The rock cycle

The **rock cycle** shows how rocks are changed and recycled in the Earth:

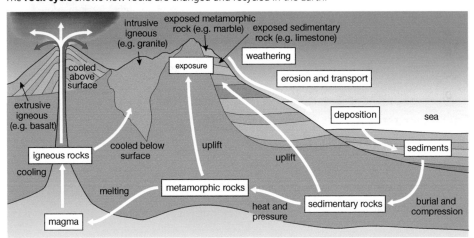

2 What is the rock cycle?

Rocks

1 Decide whether each of the following features is found in **sedimentary**, **metamorphic** or **igneous rocks** by putting a tick in the correct column(s).

	Sedimentary	Metamorphic	Igneous
a) fossils			
b) layers			
c) crystals			
d) grains			
e) solid at room temperature			

2 **a)** Give an example of a sedimentary rock.

b) Give an example of a metamorphic rock.

c) Give an example of an igneous rock.

The rock cycle

3 **a)** Describe how igneous rocks are formed.

b) Describe how sedimentary rocks are formed.

c) Describe how metamorphic rocks are formed.

What is a distance-time graph?

A distance-time graph representing a journey

A journey can be shown on a graph, known as a **distance-time graph**. For example:

- A car journey involves travelling on two motorways. The first is very busy so the driver decides to keep to one lane and maintains the car's speed at a steady 80 km per hour (50 mph).
- After 15 minutes, the driver transfers to another motorway, which has less traffic. He accelerates the car up to 112 km/h and maintains this steady speed for 15 minutes.
- He then reduces the car's speed, leaves the motorway by the exit road, and parks at a service station.

> The distance-time graph shows the distance the car has travelled as time passes, measured from the starting point.

On the graph:
- an inclined straight line shows the car travelling at a steady speed
- a steeper inclined straight line shows the car travelling at a faster steady speed
- a line getting steeper shows **acceleration**
- a line getting less steep shows **deceleration**
- a horizontal line shows the car is stationary.

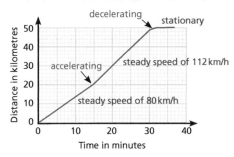

The car travels a total distance of 50 km in a total time of 32 minutes (= 0.533 hours). During the journey, there were changes in the car's **actual speed** but the car's **average speed** for the journey can be calculated from the equation:

average speed = total distance ÷ total time = 50 ÷ 0.533 = 94 km/h

Relative speed

During the first 15 minutes of the journey shown above, the driver was travelling at a steady speed of 80 km/h. A car passed him travelling at a steady speed of 90 km/h. Both cars were moving fast, but the other car appeared to the driver to be passing him slowly. This effect is due to their **relative motion**.

> For objects travelling in the same direction: **relative speed = fastest speed - slowest speed**
> So, the relative speed for the two cars = 90 - 80 = 10 km/h

At one point during the journey, the driver was travelling at a steady speed of 112 km/h in the outside lane. Another car was travelling in the outside lane on the other side of the motorway, also at 112 km/h. Because of their relative motion, the other car appeared to be travelling at a very high speed.

> For objects travelling in opposite directions: **relative speed = fastest speed + slowest speed**
> So, the relative speed for the two cars = 112 + 112 = 224 km/h

What is a distance–time graph?

A distance–time graph representing a journey

1 Two friends go on a cycle ride together for 140 minutes. The distance–time graph represents their journey.

a) Describe the cyclists' motion at each time specified.

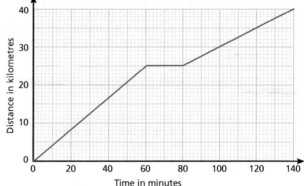

i) At time = 40 mins:

....

....

ii) At time = 70 mins:

....

....

iii) At time = 120 mins:

....

....

b) Which is greater: their speed at 20 minutes or their speed at 100 minutes?

....

c) i) What is their total distance travelled after 140 minutes? .... km

ii) What is 140 minutes in hours? .... hours

iii) Calculate the average speed for their journey in kilometres per hour.

.... km/h

Relative speed

2 A cyclist is travelling at 22 km/h. A car overtakes at a speed of 50 km/h.

Calculate the relative speed of the cyclist and the car.

.... km/h

3 Two trains on different tracks are both travelling in opposite directions at 70 km/h.

Calculate their relative speed.

.... km/h

What happens when forces are balanced?

Balanced forces on stationary objects

Forces are balanced when objects are stationary. Two examples are given below:
- A lift has just stopped and the doors have opened. The total downward force on the lift is equal to the weight of the lift and the weight of the people inside. There is an upward force created by the tension in the lift cable. The lift is stationary so the forces on the lift are **balanced**.

> An object on which the forces are balanced is described as being in **equilibrium**.

- The van is parked on a slope. There are contact forces, friction forces, and the force of gravity acting on the van. The van remains stationary, so all these forces are balanced. The van is in equilibrium. The large friction force on the van's back wheels is created by the van's handbrake. If the handbrake failed, the van would start to roll down the slope, gaining speed. The forces are no longer balanced so the van is now not in equilibrium.

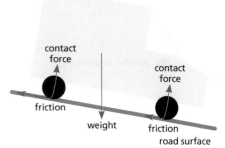

Balanced forces on moving objects

Forces can also be balanced when objects are moving. Two examples are given below:
- A parachutist is falling at a steady speed of 30 km/h. There are two forces acting on the parachutist. The parachute exerts an upward force due to air resistance. The force of gravity (her weight) acts downwards.
  The parachutist is in equilibrium. So, if her weight is 600 N, the air resistance must also be 600 N.

> If there is no change to the motion of an object, the forces acting must be balanced, and the object is in equilibrium.

- The van is in equilibrium because it is travelling along a flat road at a steady speed. The forces on the van are either vertical or horizontal. Vertical forces are the weight and the contact forces; these three forces are balanced. Horizontal forces are friction, air resistance, and driving force from the van's engine; these three forces are balanced.
  So, if the driving force is 800 N, the friction and the air resistance must add up to 800 N.

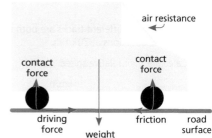

What happens when forces are balanced?

Balanced forces on stationary objects

1 An apple hangs by its stem from a branch of a tree.

   a) Complete the sentence:

      The apple is stationary so the forces acting on it are balanced and the apple is in

      ....

   b) The weight of the apple is 1 N. What is the tension in the stem?

      .... N

2 A mass is suspended by a newton-meter.
The mass and newton-meter are stationary.

   a) Name the **two** forces that are balanced.

      ....

      ....

   b) Give the direction and size of the two balanced forces.

      ....

      ....

Balanced forces on moving objects

3 A cable attached to a crane lifts
a 20,000 N load at a steady speed.

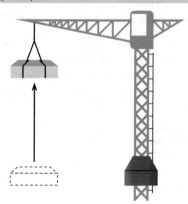

   a) Complete the sentence:

      Since the load is being lifted at a steady speed, it must be in equilibrium, and the forces acting

      on it must be ....

   b) Give the name, direction, and size of both forces acting on the load:

      ....

      ....

3 How do planets move in space?

The Earth and the Moon

The image shows a view of the Earth from the Moon. The Earth's mass is about 80 times bigger than the Moon's mass. The gravitational force between the Earth and the Moon keeps the Moon in orbit around the Earth.

Your mass is determined by how much matter makes up your body. Your **weight** is the force of gravity exerted on you by whichever astronomical body you are standing on:
- an astronaut of mass 70 kg standing on the Moon has a weight of 112 N
- this is about 6 times smaller than his weight on Earth
- his weight is smaller on the Moon because the Moon's gravitational field strength is weaker.

Weight (W), mass (m) and gravitational field strength (g) are connected by the equation: **W = mg**

> Gravitational field strength (g) is the weight of a mass of 1 kilogram.

In July 1969, NASA's Apollo 11 mission landed on the Moon and the astronauts were the first to walk on the Moon. They left mirrors on the Moon's surface so that NASA could fire laser beams at them. They measured the time for the light in the beam to travel to the Moon and back to Earth as about 2.5 s. This is a round trip of about 770,000 km.

The Solar System

The Earth orbits the Sun at a speed of about 30 kilometres per second, or 67,000 miles per hour. In the diagram, the red arrow represents the force of gravity exerted by the Sun on the Earth. This force keeps the Earth in its orbit. The distance from the Sun to the Earth is 150 million kilometres.

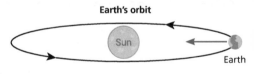

Earth's orbit

Sun

Earth

It takes just over 8 minutes for light to travel from the Sun to Earth.

The image shows the planets of the Solar System in orbit around the Sun.

> The Sun's gravitational field exerts forces on the planets to keep them in their orbits.

- The time for light to travel from Neptune to the Earth is about 4 hours.
- The nearest star to the Solar System is Proxima Centauri.
- It takes light just over 4 years to travel from Proxima Centauri to Earth.

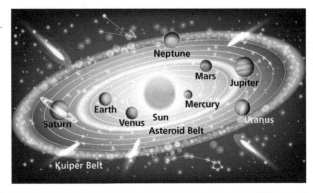

> Scientists use the distance travelled by light in one year as a unit to measure the huge distances in space. So, the distance to Proxima Centauri is 4.25 light-years, written as 4.25 ly.

How do planets move in space?

The Earth and the Moon

1 **a)** What determines the mass of an object?

....

b) The gravitational field strength at the Earth's surface is about 10 N/kg. Explain what this means.

....

c) An astronaut has a mass of 60 kg. Calculate the astronaut's weight if he was standing on the Moon.
The gravitational field strength on the Moon is 1.6 N/kg. .... N

2 In one orbit of the Earth, the Moon travels about 2,400,000 kilometres. It takes 656 hours (about 27 days) to complete one orbit of the Earth. What is the Moon's orbital speed in kilometres per hour? (Use the equation: speed = distance ÷ time) Tick **one** box.

2700 km/h ☐   3700 km/h ☐   4700 km/h ☐

The Solar System

3 **a)** The Earth completes one orbit of the Sun in 365 days. Would you expect Jupiter to take more time or less time to complete one orbit of the Sun? Explain your answer.

....

b) Planets move very fast in their orbit around the Sun. Why don't they fly off into space?

....

4 Scientists prefer to measure distances in space in light-years.

a) What is meant by 1 light-year?

....

b) A distance of 1 light-year is about 10,000,000,000,000 km. Why do you think scientists prefer to use light-years instead of kilometres?

....

5 The image represents the Milky Way galaxy. The position of the Solar System is shown by the red dot. At the centre of the Milky Way is a massive black hole. The Solar System is about 25,000 ly from the centre of the Milky Way. An object near the centre is viewed by an astronomer using a powerful telescope.

a) How long does it take for light from the object to reach Earth?

....

b) How far back in time does the image seen by the astronomer actually correspond to the object's appearance?

....

3 How does the Earth's motion affect us?

The effect of the Earth's rotation

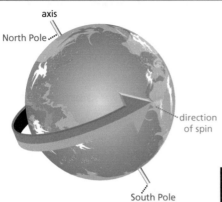

axis

North Pole

direction of spin

South Pole

The Earth spins. This spinning motion is called the **Earth's rotation**. The Earth's axis of rotation is an imaginary line between the North and South Poles. One rotation takes 24 hours. This means that the Earth's surface is moving. It moves fastest at the equator but decreases as you approach the Poles. For example, the surface speed at the latitude of London is about 1000 km/h. The surface speed at the latitude of the arctic circle is about 700 km/h. We cannot sense this rotation speed because we are rotating with the Earth.

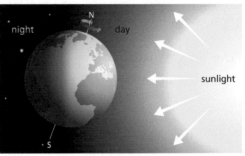

night   N   day

sunlight

S

When our part of the Earth is facing the Sun it is daytime. But as the Earth rotates, our part of the Earth is no longer illuminated by the Sun, and it is night-time.

> The Earth's rotation creates day and night.

The effect of the Earth's orbital motion around the Sun

The Earth completes one orbit of the Sun in 365.25 days. The Earth's rotation axis is slightly tilted compared with the way the Earth orbits the Sun.

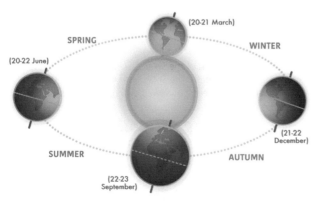

(20-21 March)

SPRING   WINTER

(20-22 June)

(21-22 December)

SUMMER   AUTUMN

(22-23 September)

> The seasons are caused by the tilt of the Earth's rotation axis.

The seasons labelled on the diagram correspond to the northern hemisphere:

- In the summer, the Earth's northern hemisphere tilts towards the Sun. This means that the Sun is higher in the sky and the sunlight travels directly to the Earth's surface.

- In the winter, the Earth's northern hemisphere tilts away from the Sun, which appears lower in the sky. Sunlight is spread out more so less energy per square metre is transferred to the Earth's surface.

③ How does the Earth's motion affect us?

The effect of the Earth's rotation

1 All points on the Earth's surface complete one rotation in 24 hours. Consider a point on the equator. During one rotation, the point on the equator moves in a circle of circumference 40,000 km.

a) What is the speed of a point on the equator due to the Earth's rotation? Tick **one** box.

1700 km/h ☐   2700 km/h ☐   3700 km/h ☐

b) Consider a point on the Earth's surface that is midway between the equator and the North Pole.

Would you expect this point to travel faster or slower or the same as the speed you calculated in part a)? Explain your answer.

....

....

2 Using the words in the box, complete the sentences to explain day and night.

light	dark	east	west	daytime	night-time

The Sun appears to rise in the east and set in the .... This effect is caused by

the rotation of the Earth about its axis, in a direction from west to .... When

the Sun lights up half of the Earth, the other half is .... In the half that is lit

up, it is .... In the half that is dark, it is .... As the

Earth continues to rotate, we move from dark to .... and back to

.... and so on.

The effect of the Earth's orbital motion around the Sun

3 The diagram shows the Earth moving in its orbit around the Sun; the Moon orbiting the Earth and the Earth's rotation.

a) Complete the sentences with the corresponding times. Include units in your answers.

i) Time taken for the Earth to complete one

orbit of the Sun = ...

ii) Time taken for the Moon to complete one

orbit of the Earth = ...

iii) Time taken for the Earth to complete one rotation about its axis = ...

b) Does the image represent summer or winter in the northern hemisphere? Explain your answer.

....

What are stars?

The Sun

- The Sun is a ball of gas held together by its own gravity.
- The Sun's surface temperature is about 6000°C. At its core, the temperature is much higher, about 15 million°C.
- The Sun radiates a lot of energy, which is generated in the core where **nuclear reactions** convert mass to energy.
- The Sun's mass is mostly made up of **hydrogen and helium**. These elements are involved in the nuclear reactions generating the energy that life on Earth relies upon.
- The Sun is a stable star and will remain stable for at least another 5 billion years.

> The Sun was created in a gas cloud, called a **nebula**, about 5 billion years ago.

Stars

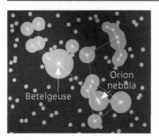

The image shows the **constellation** of Orion. It is easily seen in the northern hemisphere during winter if you look in the southern sky. On a very clear night, you can see what looks like three stars close together, but the middle one is not actually a star; it is a gas cloud called the Orion nebula, where new stars are being created.

Stars are born with masses that are about a tenth of the Sun's mass up to 200 times as massive. The more massive the star, the shorter the time it spends as a stable star. Betelgeuse is 11 times more massive than the Sun. It is no longer stable and has swollen up to be over 700 times wider than the Sun. It is described as a **red supergiant**.

In 2019 the Hubble Space Telescope observed Betelgeuse experience a huge explosion, resulting in the loss of part of its surface. At some point in its future, Betelgeuse will explode as a **supernova**, leaving a remnant that is either a **neutron star** or a **black hole**. The Sun's mass is not big enough for it to explode as a supernova.

> The Sun will eventually become a red giant, blow away its outer layers, and become a white dwarf star.

Galaxies

Stars live in 'star cities' called **galaxies**, which have a variety of shapes and sizes. Some galaxies change shape over time, possibly due to collisions with other galaxies.

To find out how galaxies first formed we need to look back in time. The more distant the object you view with a telescope, the further back in time you are observing. Hubble has seen as far back as 12.9 billion years. The James Webb Space Telescope will look even further back in time.

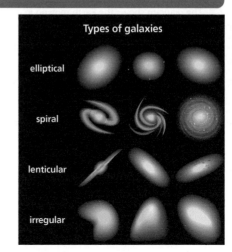

Types of galaxies

elliptical

spiral

lenticular

irregular

> Our galaxy, the **Milky Way**, is a spiral galaxy, with a super-massive black hole at its centre.

What are stars?

The Sun

1 **a)** Which **two** chemical elements make up most of the matter in the Sun?

....

b) The Sun is a ball of gas. What holds the Sun's gas particles together?

....

c) What type of reactions generate the energy that the Sun radiates?

....

d) What is the name given to a gas cloud in which stars are created?

....

e) Approximately how long ago was the Sun created?

.... years

Stars

2 **a)** The Sun will continue to be a stable star for about 5 billion years. Describe what will happen to the Sun when it is no longer a stable star.

....

....

b) Rigel is a star in the Orion constellation that is even brighter than Betelgeuse. Rigel is 21 times more massive than the Sun and is described as a blue supergiant star. Rigel will eventually explode as a supernova.

What are the **two** possible remnants left after its supernova explosion?

....

Galaxies

3 **a)** What type of galaxy is the Milky Way?

....

b) What is at the centre of the Milky Way?

....

4 The nearest large galaxy to the Milky Way is Andromeda. It is 2.5 million light-years away from us.

a) What type of galaxy is Andromeda?

....

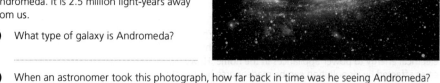

b) When an astronomer took this photograph, how far back in time was he seeing Andromeda?

....

⟨3⟩ What are waves?

Wave properties

The image shows the effect of raindrops falling on to a deep puddle. When a raindrop hits the water, some of its **kinetic energy** is transferred across the water surface by a **wave**.
The wave travels horizontally outwards from the point where the raindrop hits the water, creating the pattern of circles. The water just moves up and down. This type of wave is described as **transverse**.

> A wave is a disturbance that travels from one point to another, transferring energy.

- Where the water level is raised is a **crest**.
- Where the water level is lowered is a **trough**.
- The number of waves passing a given point in a second is the wave **frequency**.

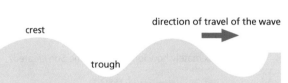

crest

trough

direction of travel of the wave

Where two raindrops hit the puddle at about the same time, the waves created can be seen passing through each other. When a crest from one wave passes through a crest from another wave, a crest of double the height is produced. Similarly, when two troughs pass through each other they make a much deeper trough. But when a crest and a trough meet, they cancel each other so the water is not disturbed.

> The effect produced when two waves pass through each other is called **superposition**.

The table shows some properties of light, sound, and surface water waves.

Wave	Transverse	Longitudinal	Carries energy	Can travel through a vacuum	Can be reflected
Light	✓	✗	✓	✓	✓
Sound	✗	✓	✓	✗	✓
Water surface	✓	✗	✓	✗	✓

Energy transfer by light

On Earth, our main light source is the Sun:
- Sunlight transfers energy from the Sun to the Earth.
- We can feel warmed by sunlight, and sunlight on our skin can create vitamin D, needed for good health, but too much sunlight can damage the cells in our skin.
- A plant can transfer energy from sunlight to its chemical energy store, which enables it to grow. This is called **photosynthesis**.

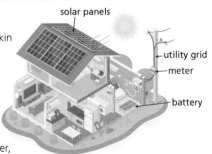

solar panels

utility grid

meter

battery

Scientists have created **photovoltaic cells** in the form of solar panels that can transfer energy from sunlight to electrical energy to power appliances in the home. However, cities affected by air pollution can be made worse by sunlight causing chemical reactions. These produce a **photochemical smog** which is hazardous to health.

What are waves?

Wave properties

1 The image shows a snapshot of a wave produced by moving one end of a long slinky up and down. The full length of the slinky is not shown, and the far end (to the right) is fixed.

disturbance direction

travel direction

Y

spring

X

a) **i)** Name the part of the wave shown at X. ....

ii) Name the part of the wave shown at Y. ....

b) Explain the meaning of wave frequency.

....

c) Is the wave on the slinky transverse or longitudinal? ....

d) When the wave reaches the fixed end, it is reflected back along the spring. So now two waves are travelling back and forth along the spring.

What is the name given to the effect of two waves passing through each other?

....

2 **a)** Give **one** way in which light waves and sound waves are different to each other.

....

b) Give **one** way in which light waves and sound waves are similar.

....

Energy transfer by light

3 The image shows solar panels in a farmer's field.

a) What is the name given to the cells inside the solar panels?

....

b) Describe the energy transfer that takes place inside the cells in the solar panels.

....

c) Sunlight is also absorbed by the grass in the farmer's field. What is the name given to the process by which energy transferred by sunlight increases the grass's chemical energy?

....

What is reflection?

Reflection of light

The photo shows a sharp reflected image of the buildings by the lake. The water in the lake is perfectly still and is acting like a mirror.

> Reflection of light by a mirror is called **specular reflection**.

If the water became choppy, it would no longer act like a mirror and the reflected image of the buildings would disappear. This is because the rays of light incident on the choppy water surface would be reflected in different directions.

Specular reflection

incident rays   reflected rays

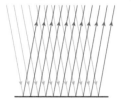

water surface acting like a mirror

Diffuse scattering

choppy surface of the water

> Reflection of light by an uneven surface is called **diffuse scattering**.

When you look in a mirror, your image appears to be behind the mirror. Of course, it isn't really behind the mirror, so it is described as a **virtual image**.

A flat mirror is also known as a **plane mirror**. Your image in a plane mirror is upright and the same height as you. But if you raise your right hand, the image's left hand is raised.

> The right side of an object appears on the left side of the image created by a plane mirror.

Transmission of light

Transparent
ALL light passes through

Translucent
SOME light passes through

Opaque
NO light passes through

An object is **transparent** if it allows light to pass straight through. In this case there is no interaction between the light and the molecules that form the object.

An object is **translucent** if some light passes through and some light interacts with the object's molecules. Two possible interactions with molecules include being absorbed and being scattered off into other directions.

An **opaque** object does not allow light to pass through. The light is either reflected or absorbed by the object's molecules.

> The passage of light through an object depends on whether there are interactions between the light and the object's molecules.

③ What is reflection?

Reflection of light

1 The image shows light from an object hitting a plane mirror.

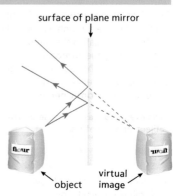

surface of plane mirror

virtual image

object

a) What is the name given to the type of reflection shown?

....

....

b) Describe **one** difference and **one** similarity between the virtual image and the object.

....

....

....

....

....

2 The image shows light being reflected from a rough surface.

rough surface

What is the name of this effect?

....

Transmission of light

3 What happens to light when it hits a transparent object?

....

4 Identify each object as **transparent**, **translucent**, or **opaque**.

a) A frosted glass window is ....

b) A ceramic vase is ....

c) An ice cube is ....

5 Describe how the molecules of an opaque object interact with light.

....

3 How do we see?

The human eye

The diagram shows two rays of light entering the eye through a hole in the iris. This hole is called the **pupil**. The light is bent by the **cornea** and the lens and focused on the **retina**. Information collected by the retina is transferred to the brain via the **optic nerve**.

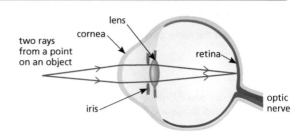

The eye produces an image of the object on the retina.

Luminous and non-luminous objects

- An object that emits its own light is called a **luminous object**. For example: a candle, a light bulb, a star.
- An object that does not emit its own light is called a **non-luminous object**. It can only be seen by reflected light. For example: a book, a person, a planet.
- Light from the candle flame (a luminous object) travels directly to the eye.
- Light from the candle also hits the book. The book (a non-luminous object) reflects the light into the eye.

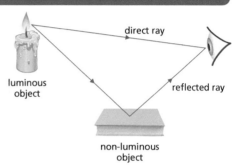

A luminous object is seen by the light it emits. A non-luminous object is seen by the light it reflects.

How do we see colour?

We know from observing rainbows that sunlight is made up of several colours: red, orange, yellow, green, blue, indigo, and violet. Experiments show that white light from a torch or lamp is also made up of this **spectrum** of colours.

The different colours of light have different wavelengths, with red having the longest.

A torch emits a beam of light, which appears white, but we know it is made up of different colours. It is shone on a book in a darkened room. The book appears red, because the molecules of the book cover absorb all the colours in the beam except red, which is reflected into our eyes.

Cells in the retina can detect red, green, and blue light.

We can create a beam of red light by putting a red plastic filter in front of the torch. Only red light can pass through the filter.

The molecules in a red filter absorb all the colours in a beam of white light except red, which is able to pass through.

③ How do we see?

The human eye

1 **a)** Look at the diagram of the human eye. Give the letter that labels each of these parts of the eye.

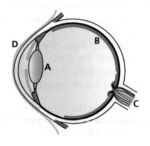

   i) retina ☐

   ii) lens ☐

   iii) cornea ☐

   iv) optic nerve ☐

   b) What is the name of the hole in the iris through which light from an object can enter the eye?

   ....

   c) Light from an object enters the eye and is refracted by the lens and the cornea to form an image. On which part of the eye is the image formed?

   ....

   d) How does information about the image formed in the eye reach the brain?

   ....

Luminous and non-luminous objects

2 **a)** What is the difference between a luminous object and a non-luminous object?

   ....

   ....

   b) **i)** The following list contains luminous and non-luminous objects. Circle the **three** luminous objects.

star	book	chair	candle flame	glass	fire	wall

   ii) Explain how it is possible to see a non-luminous object.

   ....

   ....

How do we see colour?

3 White light is made up of several colours. Name **three** of them.

....

....

③ What is refraction?

Refraction of light

The diagram shows an experiment in which a student directs a red laser beam at a rectangular block of glass. He observes that:

- the laser beam changes direction when it travels from the air into the glass
- the beam bends back to the original direction when it comes out of the glass into the air.

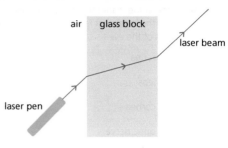

> The change of direction of a light beam as it crosses a boundary between two transparent materials is called **refraction**.

The diagram shows the light beam at the point where it first enters the glass. Light is a transverse wave, so the laser beam is represented by rows of crests.

- As the laser beam enters the glass, its speed decreases.
- The part of one row of crests in the glass moves more slowly than another part, still in the air, which causes the laser beam to bend.
- Light travels more slowly in glass than air because glass is much denser.
- When the laser beam re-enters the air, it speeds up again.

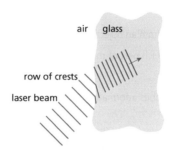

> The refraction of light is caused by a change in its speed.

A solid triangular piece of glass is called a **prism**. When a laser beam is incident on a prism, refraction causes the beam to change direction. Because the sides of the prism are not parallel, the refraction on leaving the prism bends the beam even more.

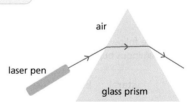

Refraction producing a spectrum of colours

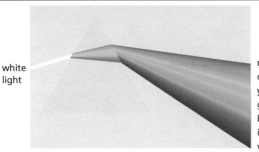

white light

red
orange
yellow
green
blue
indigo
violet

A beam of white light is made up of a spectrum of colours. When the beam is directed at a prism, the different colours are refracted by different amounts.

> A prism refracts a beam of white light to produce a **visible spectrum**. This effect is called **dispersion**.

③ What is refraction?

Refraction of light

1 A laser beam is directed at a rectangular glass block. The beam is refracted at the boundary between the air and the glass.

a) How does the speed of the laser beam change as it travels from the air into the glass?

....

b) How does the speed of the laser beam change as it travels from the glass back into the air?

....

c) Draw a line to show the path of the laser beam as it emerges from the glass block.

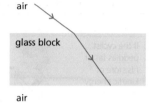

air

glass block

air

2 A ray of light (shown in red) travels from the fish to the water surface. The ray bends at the water surface and continues into the person's eye (shown as a dotted red line).

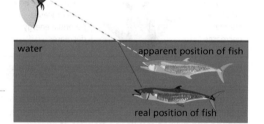

air

water

apparent position of fish

real position of fish

a) i) What is the name given to the bending of a ray of light as it travels from the water into the air?

....

ii) What causes the bending of the ray of light?

....

b) Does the refraction at the water surface make the pond appear deeper or shallower than it really is? ....

Refraction producing a spectrum of colours

3 A combination of sunshine and showers produces a rainbow. The diagram represents a ray of sunlight incident on a raindrop.

a) On the diagram, mark an X wherever there is refraction of the light.

b) On the diagram, mark a Y wherever there is reflection of the light.

c) What is the scientific name given for the rainbow of colours?

....

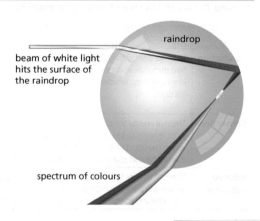

raindrop

beam of white light hits the surface of the raindrop

spectrum of colours

How does energy transfer?

Energy stores and transfers

Energy is never created, or lost, it is just transferred between energy stores. This is known as the **Law of Conservation of Energy**. For example, suppose a change takes place, causing energy to be transferred from one store to another: if the first energy store decreases by 100 J, the second energy store increases by 100 J.

The five main energy stores are shown below:

Kinetic energy store	Thermal energy store	Chemical energy store
If the cyclist peddles faster, his store of kinetic energy increases.	The poker's store of thermal energy increases when it is put into the fire.	Chemical energy is transferred if the battery is connected into a circuit or if the coal is ignited.

Gravitational potential energy store	Elastic potential energy store	
As the skydiver falls, her store of gravitational potential energy decreases.	When the archer fires the arrow, the bow's store of elastic potential energy decreases.	**Energy can be transferred between stores by a force, by heating, by an electric current or by a wave.**

Energy transfer by heating

The sequence of energy transfers when a portable gas stove heats water in an aluminium can is shown. The chemical reaction involving combustion of propane and oxygen results in a transfer of energy.

Chemical energy stored in propane and oxygen → Combustion of propane and oxygen transfers chemical energy to thermal energy → Thermal energy transferred by a temperature difference →
- Thermal energy store of aluminium can increases
- Thermal energy store of water increases
- Thermal energy store of surroundings increases

The transfer of thermal energy because of a difference in temperature is usually referred to as heating. Details of the three heating processes are shown in the table below:

Process	Method	Medium
Conduction	Thermal energy transferred through a material or between two materials in contact: particles at the hot end gain kinetic energy, which is transferred to neighbouring particles.	All materials conduct thermal energy but solids, especially metals, are the best thermal conductors, e.g. a metal spoon getting warm when stirring hot soup in a pan on the stove.
Convection	Thermal energy transferred through a liquid or gas: particles in a hot space gain kinetic energy and push each other further apart. The liquid or gas in the hot space becomes less dense than in the cold space, so it rises, flowing into the cold space.	Works in liquids and gases because these can flow. Does not work in solids, e.g. a hot air balloon rising.
Infrared radiation	Thermal energy transferred by infrared radiation: all objects radiate infrared radiation and the higher the object's temperature, the greater the amount of infrared emitted.	No particles involved so can transfer energy through a vacuum, e.g. thermal energy transferred from the Sun to Earth.

How does energy transfer?

Energy stores and transfers

1 The stem of an apple breaks. The force of gravity acting on the apple causes it to fall from the tree resulting in a transfer of energy.

a) Name the energy store that is decreasing.

....

....

b) Name the energy store that is increasing as the apple falls.

....

....

2 A car driver applies the brakes on seeing a hazard in the road ahead. The force of friction brings the car to a stop and raises the temperature of the brakes.

a) Describe the energy store that has decreased.

....

b) Describe the energy store that has increased.

....

Energy transfer by heating

3 The incomplete flow chart represents energy changes when a torch is switched on. Fill in the missing words.

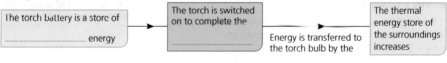

| The torch battery is a store of .... energy | The torch is switched on to complete the .... | Energy is transferred to the torch bulb by the | The thermal energy store of the surroundings increases |

....

....

4 a) Which heating process occurs most effectively in solids? ....

b) Which heating process can transfer energy through a vacuum? ....

c) Which heating process occurs in liquids and gases but not in solids? ....

How do we compare energy transfer?

Energy transferred when eating

Any food item is a **chemical energy store**. A packaged food item usually contains a label showing the amount of energy it stores. For example, a packet of crisps is a store of about 500 kJ.

> 1 kilojoule is equal to 1000 joules.

- Some food labels quote the energy transferred per 100 grams, e.g. the label on a bag of potatoes would typically be '320 kJ of energy per 100 g'. If you ate a jacket potato that had a mass of 200 g prior to cooking, the energy transferred to you = 320 x 2 = 640 kJ.

- When a person eats a food item, its energy store is transferred by many chemical reactions, enabling the person's body to function and store energy.
- Different activities transfer different amounts of energy, e.g. walking transfers approximately 880–1500 kJ per hour, sleeping transfers approximately 200 kJ per hour, so if you slept for 8 hours, the total energy transferred = 200 × 8 = 1600 kJ.

Energy transferred by appliances in the home

> An electrical appliance transfers energy stored in the mains electrical supply to other energy stores.

When you switch on an electric kettle, an electric current flows through its heating element, transferring energy from the mains. The energy transfer increases the thermal energy stores of the water in the kettle, the body of the kettle, and its surroundings.

> The **power** of an electrical appliance is the energy it transfers in 1 second.

> 1 joule of energy transferred in 1 second represents a power of 1 watt, written as 1 W.

Household electrical appliances are labelled with their **power**. The label on a hairdryer shows that its power is 800 W, meaning that it transfers 800 J of energy from the mains supply every second.

> power = energy ÷ time
>
> in watts   in joules   in seconds

Rearranging the power equation to make energy the subject gives:
energy = power × time

If the hairdryer was used for 5 minutes, how much energy would it transfer? First convert 5 minutes to seconds, so time = 5 × 60 = 300 seconds.

> 1 kilowatt (1 kW) is equal to 1000 watts.

Now use the energy equation, so energy transferred = 800 × 300 = 240,000 J.

The table shows the typical power of some electrical appliances.

Appliance	Power in watts
fan	45
blender	600
iron	2400

Appliances designed to produce thermal energy usually have greater powers. High powers are often given in **kilowatts (kW)**, e.g. the power of the iron may be given as 2.4 kW.

③ How do we compare energy transfer?

Energy transferred when eating

1 **a)** What type of energy store is food? ....

b) The label on a package of sausages states that two sausages provide 930 kJ of energy. What is the total energy stored in the pack?

.... kJ

2 A bag of carrots in a supermarket has a mass of 500 g. The label on the bag states that the 100 g of the carrots is an energy store of 150 kJ. How much energy is stored in the whole bag?

.... kJ

3 A hiker walks for 3 hours, transferring 1200 kilojoules per hour. He stops and eats sandwiches of total mass 300 g. The sandwich packaging states that the energy content is 800 kJ per 100 g.

a) How much energy does the hiker transfer during his walk? .... kJ

b) How much energy is supplied by his sandwiches? .... kJ

c) Does the energy supplied by the sandwiches replace the energy he transferred during the walk?

....

Energy transferred by appliances in the home

4 An electric immersion heater transfers 12,000,000 J in 25 minutes.

a) Use the equation **power = energy ÷ time** to calculate the power of the immersion heater in watts.

power = ... watts

b) Convert your answer in part a) to kilowatts: .... kW

5 The power rating on an electric kettle is 2200 W.

a) Explain what this means in terms of how quickly it transfers energy.

....

....

b) **i)** The kettle full of water takes 2½ minutes to boil. Convert 2½ minutes to seconds. .... s

ii) Use the equation **energy = power × time** to calculate how much energy is transferred by the kettle during the 2½ minutes it takes to boil the water. .... J

6 A 2 kW electric heater is switched on for 30 minutes.

a) Give the power of the heater in watts. .... W

b) Convert 30 minutes to seconds. .... s

c) How much energy does the heater transfer? .... J

Mixed questions

1 Look at the diagrams of two microbes.

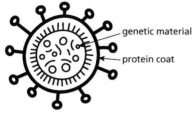

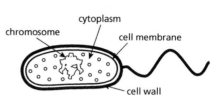

influenza microbe   **typhoid microbe**

a) Write down the type of microbe that causes each of these diseases.

Choose from **fungus, bacterium** and **virus**.

i) influenza .... **ii)** typhoid ....

b) Which of these microbes is a living cell? How can you tell from the diagram?

....

....

c) Explain why antibiotics cannot destroy both microbes.

....

....

d) How can you tell that both of these diagrams have not been drawn to the same scale?

....

2 Malachite is a copper ore which mainly contains copper carbonate.

a) Write a word equation for the thermal decomposition of copper carbonate to make carbon dioxide and another product.

....

b) Describe a simple laboratory test to show that carbon dioxide is made from the thermal decomposition of a metal carbonate.

....

....

c) Explain how industrial thermal decomposition of malachite could lead to climate change.

....

....

....

d) Explain why carbon can be used to extract copper from a compound.

....

Mixed questions

3 A car is travelling along the road at a steady speed. There are three horizontal forces acting on the car, labelled A, B, and C.

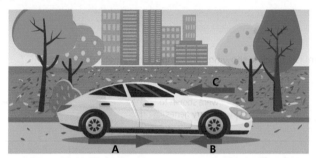

a) Force A is the driving force generated by the engine. Give the names of forces B and C.

B: ....

C: ....

b) Force B = 200N. Force C = 300N. What is the size of force A?

.... N

4 Teflon is a polymer that is used to coat non-stick pans. Look at the diagrams of Teflon below.

a) What is the yellow sphere representing?

....

b) What is the black sphere representing?

....

c) Describe the structure of a polymer.

....

....

d) Explain why this polymer is a solid at room temperature.

_____

_____

_____

5 The diagram is a timeline showing some important genetic discoveries.

1910 – Chromosomes were shown to carry genes

1996 – The first cloned mammal was born

1863 – It was realised that characteristics were passed on from both parents to children

1953 – The structure of DNA was discovered

a) Which **two** scientists built a model of DNA in 1953?

_____

b) In 1863, Mendel realised that characteristics were passed on from both parents to children. However, he did not know how the characteristics were passed on.

Use the timeline to explain why he did not know this.

_____

_____

6 A blue plastic filter is placed in front of a torch emitting a beam of white light.

beam of blue light

blue filter

a) What happens to the colours in the beam of white light when it hits the blue filter?

_____

b) Alice is wearing a jacket which appears red in daylight.

If she goes into a room where the only light source is a beam of blue light, what colour will her jacket appear?

Explain your answer.

_____

_____

Mixed questions

7 **a)** Write down the name of the scientist who first put forward the theory of natural selection.

b) The drawing shows an insect called the peppered moth.

dark peppered moth

The moth is usually light coloured and lives on trees where it is well camouflaged.

Scientists noticed that in areas where the trees became stained black by pollution, a dark form of the moth became common.

pale peppered moth

The statements, A to E, show how this can be explained by natural selection. They are not in the correct order.

A Dark moths will pass on the gene for dark colour

B Dark moths were better camouflaged in polluted areas

C Over generations, the number of dark moths will increase

D A small number of dark coloured moths are regularly produced by mutation

E Dark moths are more likely to survive in polluted areas

Write a letter in each box to show the correct order of the statements in the process of natural selection.

One has been done for you.

☐ ☐ ☐ ☐ **C**

8 The picture shows a drone. When the circuit inside the drone is completed, energy is transferred from the battery to its propellors, enabling it to take off vertically.

a) What type of energy store is the drone's battery?

b) What transfers energy from the battery to the motor to drive the propellors?

c) Name **two** of the drone's energy stores that increase during take-off.

Scientific skills

What is a conclusion?

In an **investigation, data** is collected. A researcher will look at the data and think about what it shows. They try to find a **conclusion**. A good conclusion:
* describes the relationship between the **independent variable** (the variable you choose to change) and the **dependent variable** (the variable you measure in the experiment)
* is clearly structured
* is explained using scientific knowledge
* links back to the question you want to answer in the investigation, and the **hypothesis** (what you think will happen).

Relationships in data

Relationships in numerical data can be described by a **line of best fit** on a graph. **Correlation** happens when changing the independent variable shows a change in the dependent variable. Linear correlation can be shown with a straight line of best fit.

Correlation

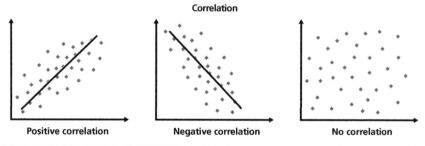

| **Positive correlation** | **Negative correlation** | **No correlation** |

> Sometimes there is no correlation in the data, in which case you should not draw a line of best fit. This means there is no relationship between the independent and dependent variables that you have chosen.

The relationship between the independent and dependent variables can be described as **directly proportional** if:
* they produce a straight-line graph, which passes through the origin (0,0)
* the dependent variable doubles when the independent variable has been doubled.

The graph below shows that the extension is directly proportional to the force.

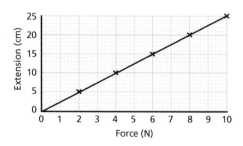

Scientific skills

What are errors?

In any investigations there may be errors that produce a difference between the collected data and the accurate or true value. Researchers must carefully consider the errors and think about whether this makes the data misleading or if it is **valid** enough to be used to find a conclusion.

Random errors

A **random error** is an error that changes each time the observation is made. This means:
- they are impossible to predict
- they can cause a large range or spread in the data
- they can produce anomalous results.

Random errors can be due to the researcher using the equipment incorrectly. For example, this could include not reading a scale directly in your eye-line.

Parallax error

Wrong reading   Right reading   Wrong reading

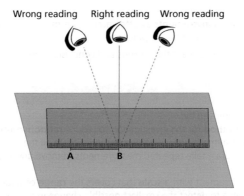

Systematic errors

A **systematic error** is an error that is the same each time the observation is made. This means:
- a measurement will not be close to the true value
- they are possible to correct in the data.

Systematic errors are often due to the equipment not being **calibrated** correctly. For example, this could include a zero error, when you use a balance without first setting it to zero, so it measures a mass as heavier or lighter than it actually is.

There will always be error in an investigation. But, with careful planning of a method and attention to detail during the practical, they can be minimised. As technology improves and we have more accurate measuring equipment, the size of errors will be reduced.

Scientific skills

How accurate are my results?

An **accurate result** is close to the accepted value. The accepted value could be:
- written in a text book
- found on a trusted website
- the results collected by your teacher.

The accuracy of the results depends on:
- the quality of the **measuring instruments** as often accuracy is most affected by **systematic errors**
- the skill of the researcher in completing the practical.

A researcher can determine how accurate their results and conclusions are by comparing them to the accepted value.

Maximum accuracy

Accuracy of results can be improved by:
- carefully following the **method** for the investigation to reduce **random errors**
- correcting any data for systematic errors – remember to calibrate all the measuring equipment
- using an average of the data – take repeated measurements, remove any anomalous results and calculate the **mean**
- selecting a measuring instrument with a **scale** that covers the **range** of values needed for the experiment and is also able to detect the smallest possible change in a measurement. For example, there are lots of different types of thermometers, and it is no good using a nurse's thermometer to measure the temperature of a flame as it cannot measure that high.

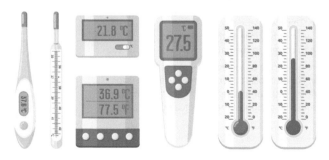

Reliable (similar each time you repeat) and accurate (close to the true value) results are the goal of a researcher.

Scientific skills

Are there limits to scientific knowledge?

Science is the study of the universe. But, there are limits to scientific knowledge because:
- it may not be possible to design an experiment to test a particular hypothesis
- data cannot be collected as the equipment does not exist – yet!
- the event has already happened and no data was collected.

Using evidence

It is not possible to go back in time and find out how the Universe began, for example, or how life on Earth started. So, scientists have to make their best guess about what happened using data that they have collected.

Sometimes, scientists get it wrong, but at the time they do not know. As technology develops, things that were not possible in the past become possible and more data can be gathered, which can be used to develop or disprove previous explanations.

Bias

Bias is when:
- one viewpoint is given, often using persuasive language
- evidence is specially selected
- data is specially collected to support a conclusion
- faulty equipment gives inaccurate results.

Bias can lead to misleading conclusions and could cause harm. Scientists reduce the likelihood of biased results and conclusions by checking each other's work before it is published. This is called **peer review** and gives confidence to the public that the information is likely to be true.

Ethics

Researchers must consider the **ethics** of their experiments. They must consider the risks and benefits and conclude that it is in humanity's best interests to complete the investigation. They should consider the consequences of their research:
- **personally** – the researcher and subjects
- **socially** – groups of people
- **economically** – costs and financial benefits
- **environmentally** – water, air and land.

> Researchers themselves often need to ask other experts like religious leaders, other scientists and the public to decide if the research is suitable to be completed. Only if the benefits equal or outweigh the risks should the research happen.

Answers

Biology

Page 5

1. a) species **b)** biodiversity **c)** classification

2. They are different species.

3.

Example	Inherited	Environment	Inherited and environment
a scar on the cheek		✓	
blood group	✓		
human height			✓
sex at birth	✓		

4. Over the years their appearances have been affected by the environment.

5. a) 36 **b)** 8 **c)** discontinuous **d)** Foot size can show a whole range of values so is continuous; shoe size has specific values.

Page 7

1. evolution; (Charles) Darwin; natural selection

2. Organisms that are best suited to their environment

3. Large muscles

4. Choose the cattle that have the most muscle/ produce the most meat, breed them together, choose the offspring that have the most muscle and continue the process.

5. Introducing foreign species; Overhunting

Page 9

1. chromosomes; genes; proteins

2.

3. double helix

4. Holds instructions about how to make proteins

5. They took photos of DNA using X-rays, which showed that DNA was made up of two chains wound up in a double helix.

6. They hold the two chains of DNA together; They code for proteins.

7. The parents will be prepared for a child that will have the disease. However, they might decide to terminate the pregnancy, which would be a difficult decision.

Page 11

1. genes/genetic material; clones

2. The plant produces long shoots called runners, which touch the soil, root and grow into new plants.

3. Identical twins are made from the embryo splitting into two so they have the same DNA. But non-identical twins are from different embryos.

4. Take a cutting by cutting off a shoot and then planting it in soil so that it can root.

5. removing a nucleus from an egg cell and replacing it with a nucleus from a body cell

6. Many elm trees reproduce asexually and so are genetically identical. This means that they will all be killed by the fungus if they are not resistant.

Page 13

1. to make them feel good/to fit in socially

2. The drug may be dangerous if taken by some people/if the wrong dose is used. The drug might be addictive.

3. cannabis – depressant – slows down breathing rate
caffeine – stimulant – increases heart rate
LSD – hallucinogen – distorts reality
morphine – painkiller – blocks pain messages

4. a) depression/possible death **b)** heart attacks

5. addiction; withdrawal effects/symptoms

6. a) Hallucinogens mean that people may see things that are not really there and so have accidents trying to avoid them.

b) Depressants make a person sleepy so they could have an accident if driving or operating machinery.

Answers

1. cannabis – tar; THC
tobacco – nicotine; tar

2. by passive smoking/from the air if near other people who are smoking

3. nicotine

4. anxiety; mental illness/schizophrenia

5. If it is eaten, the tar will not be breathed into the lungs so there is less risk of lung infections or cancer.

6. B is from the tobacco smoker, resulting in the walls of the air sacs being broken down. This will reduce the surface area, so less oxygen will pass into the blood causing less respiration.

7. Cannabis does not contain nicotine, which is addictive, but tobacco does.

8. to reduce pain or to reduce sickness if having chemotherapy

Page 17

1. It causes a person to be less shy and increases their confidence.

2. It can slow down the heart rate or breathing rate too much.

3. addiction/cirrhosis of the liver/heart disease/diabetes

4. a) $(6 \times 1.5) + 1.5 + (3 \times 2) = 16.5$ units

b) No, the limit is 14 and so they are 2.5 units over.

5. stimulants

6. Ecstasy causes an increase in body temperature, so they are trying to cool themselves down.

7. The needles may not be sterilised and so they could become infected with diseases such as HIV.

Page 19

1. a disease that can be passed on from one person to another

2. cholera – water
malaria – insect bite
influenza – air
salmonella – food

3. They contain an enzyme that kills some microbes.

4. It produces acid that kills some microbes.

5. The mucus traps microbes and contains an enzyme that kills some microbes. The cilia sweep the mucus with the trapped microbes up to the mouth.

6. People can cough or sneeze into them, preventing droplets containing the microbes being spread into the air.

7. Insecticides will kill insects such as mosquitoes, which spread the malaria microbe from person to person.

Page 21

1. Microbes are too small to be seen by the naked eye.

2. a) fungus **b)** virus

3.

Typical size in micrometres	Type of microbe
0.02	viruses
10	fungi
2	bacteria

4. AIDS – virus
thrush – fungus
cholera – bacterium
Covid – virus

5. sugar/amino acids/minerals/vitamins/water

6. to prevent them contaminating the agar with other microbes and to prevent them contracting the microbe from the Petri dish

7. 37°C, because this is normal body temperature

Page 23

1. a) An antiseptic is used on the body but a disinfectant is used on non-living material such as floors or tables.

b) An antibiotic is usually used inside the body/is made by microbes/fungi. An antiseptic is used on the outside of the body/is man-made or made by plants.

2. fungi

3. Covid is caused by a virus and antibiotics do not destroy viruses.

4. kill them; stop them from reproducing

5. D because it produces the largest clear area around the disc

Answers

6. a bacterium that is not affected by a wide range of antibiotics
7. **a)** South Korea

   b) The more antibiotics used then the higher percentage that show resistance.

Page 25

1. white; engulf; antibodies
2. **a)** It is made from a white blood cell after it has encountered a microbe.

   b) If the microbe returns to the body, then a memory cell can quickly make antibodies against it before the person becomes too ill.

3. a weakened or dead microbe
4. The virus that causes influenza changes regularly and so a new vaccination is needed to produce a new type of antibody to protect the body.
5. The vaccine might contain a weakened microbe, which might cause a very mild form of the disease.
6. to see if they protect against the disease; to see if they have any side effects; to find out what dose is needed
7. smallpox

Chemistry

Page 27

1. left and centre
2. a mixture of mainly metals to create stronger metals
3. **a)** a list of metals from most to least reactive

   b) as a comparison; to make prediction of reaction with acid and carbon easier

   c) Yes, it will react with hydrochloric acid because tin is above hydrogen in the reactivity series.
4. **a)** true **b)** false **c)** true **d)** false **e)** true
5. **a)** calcium carbonate

   b) lead oxide; carbon dioxide (in any order)

Page 29

1. mineral – a metal compound found in nature
   ore – a rock where the percentage of metal is high enough that it is financially worth extracting
   compound – more than one type of atom chemically joined
2. $(2 \div 100) \times 100 = 2\%$
3. a metal found uncombined in nature
4. **a)** false **b)** true **c)** true **d)** true **e)** false
5. **a)** Less energy is used to recycle a metal than it takes to extract a metal from its ore.

   b) Metals are finite resources and will run out. To continue to have metals, we must recycle.

Page 31

1. **a)** a chemical reaction where oxygen is lost

   b) carbon dioxide
2. coke
3. hematite
4. **a)** true **b)** false **c)** false **d)** false **e)** false
5. galena
6. *zinc sulfide*

Page 33

1. **a)** true **b)** false **c)** true **d)** true **e)** true
2. **a)** a change where energy is released to the surroundings/causes a temperature increase

   b) freezing water/metal and acid reaction/ burning a campfire
3. **a)** a change where energy is absorbed from the surroundings/causes a temperature decrease

   b) photosynthesis/cooking/thermal decomposition of metal carbonates/ neutralisation of citric acid by bicarbonate of soda
4. A = endothermic; B = exothermic
5. Use a thermometer to take the start and end temperatures. If the temperature increases, the change is exothermic. If the temperature decreases, the change is endothermic.

Page 35

1. rate of reaction – a measure of how quickly a product is made or a reactant is used up
   catalyst – a substance that changes the speed of

Answers

a chemical reaction without being used up itself
activation energy – the minimum amount of
energy to start a chemical reaction

2. 10 g

3. over the arrow

4. to make production more profitable

5. It reduces the temperature that the reaction
has to run at.

6. to change pollutant gases from a car exhaust
into gases that are naturally found in air

7. hydrocarbon + oxygen $\rightarrow$ water + carbon
dioxide

8. a) a biological catalyst

b) to make chemical reactions in organisms
fast enough to support life

Page 37

1. a) false **b)** true **c)** true **d)** false **e)** false

2. refractory – used as a heat shield on the
outside of space vehicles
structural – used to make a roofing material
whiteware – used to make pots to cook food
in and then put in the fridge to keep

3. metal oxide

4. amorphous

5. It is difficult to get the conditions correct in
every stage of the manufacture. This can
cause defects and the ceramic might not be
suitable for its job.

6. Ceramics are brittle and if dropped they will
break/shatter.

Page 39

1. a long chain molecule made from small
repeating units

2. glucose

3. protein

4. Monomers are carefully selected and heated
under great pressure with catalysts.

5. high melting and boiling point – strength of
forces between the polymer chains
density – how straight or branched the
polymer chain is
ability to form a gel – presence of cross-links

6. a) B **b)** A **c)** C

Page 41

1. They are usually stronger and more durable
than the pure substance./They have more
desirable properties than the pure substance.

2. composite – a material made from two or
more substances that have been mixed
together but are still recognisable
matrix – the main material that makes up a
composite
reinforcement – the material spread out within
the composite

3. lignin

4. calcium phosphate

5. Cermet is used to make hip replacements.

6. cement, sand and gravel/aggregate

Page 43

1. 4 billion years

2. a) carbon dioxide (CO_2)

b) photosynthesis

3. nitrogen (N_2) and oxygen (O_2)

4. There is approximately 20% oxygen and 80%
nitrogen in the atmosphere.

5. the release of harmful substances into the air

6. a) false **b)** true **c)** true **d)** false **e)** false

Page 45

1. greenhouse gas – a gas that traps solar
radiation in the atmosphere
greenhouse effect – the natural trapping of
solar radiation to keep average world
temperatures stable
global warming – the increase in average
world temperatures

2. global warming

3. reduce the amount of greenhouse gases
added to the atmosphere, e.g. reduce
combustion of fossil fuels and use more
renewable energy; remove some of the
carbon dioxide, e.g. by planting more plants
and carbon capture and storage.

4. a) true **b)** true **c)** false **d)** false **e)** true

5. units of carbon dioxide

Answers

Page 47

1. **a)** non-renewable **b)** renewable **c)** non-renewable **d)** non-renewable **e)** renewable

2. mining and quarrying

3. living as you want to today but saving some resources for people of the future to live as they want to

4. reduce, reuse, recycle

5. They are collected, separated, cleaned, melted down and re-formed into new products.

6. when the product made from recycled materials cannot then be recycled itself

7. It is more sustainable as it saves non-renewable resources, lowers carbon footprint, lowers energy consumption, lowers pollution and it is quicker than using new resources.

Page 49

1. crust – solid material made of two different densities
mantle – liquid and semi-liquid rock
core – *the centre is solid and the outside is liquid*

2. crust and the top semi-solid layer of mantle

3. crust – basalt and granite

mantle – metal and silica oxides
core – iron and nickel

4. A = outer core; B = inner core; C = crust; D = mantle

5. oceanic crust

6. about 20

7. when plates slowly move and cause the land masses to change position

Page 51

1. **a)** sedimentary; metamorphic **b)** sedimentary; metamorphic; igneous **c)** metamorphic; igneous **d)** sedimentary **e)** sedimentary; metamorphic; igneous

2. **a)** e.g. limestone or sandstone

   b) e.g. marble or slate

   c) e.g. basalt or granite

3. **a)** Molten magma or lava cools and solidifies.

   b) Rocks are weathered and transported (eroded) into sediments. Sediments settle, are compacted and then cemented together.

   c) Sedimentary rocks undergo changes due to heat and sometimes heat and pressure.

Physics

Page 53

1. **a) i)** steady speed

   ii) stationary

   iii) steady speed

   b) at 20 minutes

   c) i) 40 km

   ii) 2.33 hours

   iii) speed = distance ÷ time = 40 ÷ 2.33 = 17.2 km/h

2. relative speed = 50 – 22 = 28 km/h

3. relative speed = 70 + 70 = 140 km/h

Page 55

1. **a)** equilibrium

   b) 1 N

2. **a)** tension, weight

   b) tension: upwards, 2.2 N (accept 2.1 N);

weight: downwards, 2.2 N (accept 2.1 N)

3. **a)** balanced

   b) weight downwards 20,000 N; tension upwards 20,000 N

Page 57

1. **a)** the amount of matter in the object

   b) The force of gravity on a mass of 1 kilogram is 10 newton.

   c) (weight = 60 × 1.6 =) 96 N

2. 3700 km/h

3. **a)** It would take more time because Jupiter is further from the Sun.

   b) The Sun's gravity prevents planets flying off into space.

4. **a)** 1 light-year is the distance travelled by light in one year.

   b) Distances in space are huge.

Answers

5. a) 25,000 years

   b) 25,000 years

Page 59

1. a) 1700 km/h

   b) Slower, because a shorter distance is travelled in the same time (24 hours).

2. west; east; dark; daytime; night-time; light; dark

3. a) i) 365 years

   ii) 27 days

   iii) 24 hours

   b) Winter. The northern hemisphere is tilting away from the Sun.

Page 61

1. a) hydrogen, helium

   b) gravity

   c) nuclear reactions

   d) nebula

   e) 5 billion years

2. a) The Sun will eventually become a red giant, blow away its outer layers, and then become a white dwarf star.

   b) neutron star, black hole

3. a) spiral

   b) super-massive black hole

4. a) spiral

   b) 2.5 million years

Page 63

1. a) i) trough

   ii) crest

   b) the number of waves passing a given point in a second

   c) transverse

   d) superposition

2. a) Light is transverse, but sound is longitudinal./Light can travel through a vacuum but sound cannot.

   b) Both can transfer energy./Both can be reflected.

3. a) photovoltaic cells

   b) energy from sunlight to an electrical energy

store

   c) photosynthesis

Page 65

1. a) specular reflection

   b) Difference: left and right are reversed in the image. Similarity: same height, or same size, or both upright.

2. diffuse reflection/diffuse scattering

3. The light passes straight through.

4. a) translucent

   b) opaque

   c) translucent

5. The molecules reflect or absorb the light.

Page 67

1. a) i) B **ii)** A **iii)** D **iv)** C

   b) pupil

   c) retina

   d) by the optic nerve

2. a) A luminous object emits light. A non-luminous object does not emit light.

   b) i) star, candle flame, fire

   ii) A non-luminous object is seen by the light that it reflects.

3. Any three from: red, orange, yellow, green, blue, indigo, violet

Page 69

1. a) speed decreases

   b) speed increases

   c)

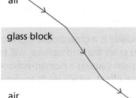

2. a) i) refraction

   ii) Light travels at different speeds in water and air. (Accept: Water is a denser medium than air.)

   b) shallower

Answers

3. a) and **b)**

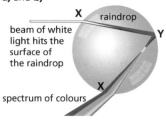

beam of white light hits the surface of the raindrop

spectrum of colours

c) visible spectrum

Page 71

1. a) the apple's gravitational potential energy store

b) the apple's kinetic energy store

2. a) the car's kinetic energy store

b) the brakes' thermal energy store

3. chemical; circuit; electric current

4. a) conduction

b) radiation

c) convection

Page 73

1. a) chemical

b) total energy = 3 × 930 = 2790 kJ

2. energy = 150 × 5 = 750 kJ

3. a) energy = 1200 × 3 = 3600 kJ

b) energy = 800 × 3 = 2400 kJ

c) no

4. a) power = 12,000,000 ÷ (25 × 60) = 8000 watts

b) 8 kW

5. a) When the kettle is switched on, 2200 J of energy is transferred every second.

b) i) 2½ × 60 = 150 seconds

ii) energy = 2200 × 150 = 330,000 J

6. a) 2000 W

b) 30 × 60 = 1800 s

c) energy = 2000 × 1800 = 3,600,000 J

Mixed questions

Pages 74–77

1. a) i) virus **ii)** bacterium

b) the typhoid microbe because it has a cell membrane and cytoplasm

c) The influenza microbe is a virus and antibiotics do not destroy viruses.

d) Bacteria are much larger than viruses.

2. a) copper carbonate → copper oxide + carbon dioxide

b) Blow through limewater, which will turn from colourless to cloudy/milky.

c) Carbon dioxide is a greenhouse gas and, if allowed to enter the atmosphere, will trap solar radiation causing a human-enhanced greenhouse effect, which leads to climate change.

4. a) fluorine atoms

b) carbon atoms

c) many repeating units (monomers) joined together to make a very long molecule

d) The long polymer chains have a high number of forces between the chains, which attract the chains to each other and give the material a high melting point.

5. a) Watson and Crick

b) Characteristics are passed on by genes and genes were not discovered until 1910.

6. a) All colours, except blue, are absorbed by the filter.

b) The jacket will appear black because it absorbs the blue light.

7. a) Charles Darwin

b) D, B, E, A, C

8. a) chemical energy store

b) the electric current

c) gravitational potential energy store and kinetic energy store